The Active/Ethical Professional

The Active/Ethical Professional

A Framework for Responsible Educators

Michael G. Gunzenhauser

continuum

Continuum International Publishing Group
80 Maiden Lane, Suite 704, New York, NY 10038
The Tower Building, 11 York Road, London SE1 7NX

www.continuumbooks.com

© Michael G. Gunzenhauser, 2012

Library of Congress Cataloging-in-Publication Data
A catalog record for this book is available from the Library of Congress.

ISBN: HB: 978-1-4411-3212-3
ISBN: PB: 978-1-4411-5210-7

Typeset by Newgen Imaging Systems Pvt Ltd, Chennai, India
Printed and bound in the United States of America

To Lynda Stone and Robert Nash

CONTENTS

PREFACE

The object was to learn to what extent the effort to think one's own history can free thought from what it silently thinks, and so enable it to think differently.

(FOUCAULT, 1985/1984, p. 9)

In public education in the United States, the call for thinking differently about educational practice is long overdue. As I complete this text in the Fall of 2011, change is happening rapidly in school districts, state policy, and federal policy. The immediate future is unknown, as a mix of reforms—privatization, charters, cyber schools, value-added assessments, and accountability policy revisions—are floating about amid dramatic state-level funding cuts and collective bargaining restrictions. The US Congress and Senate are working on their own competing versions of the reauthorization of the *Elementary and Secondary Education Act (No Child Left Behind,* [107th Congress, 2002], in its most recent iteration). As the goal of 100 percent proficiency by 2014 looms and educators and policy makers face that goal's impossibility, Secretary of Education Arne Duncan is concerned that, unless the law is rewritten more sensibly, 80 percent of the nation's schools will not meet proficiency standards this year. Duncan has promised to waive NCLB proficiency requirements for states that adopt educational reforms that the Department of Education favors, drawing the ire of Republican congressmen (Dillon, 2011).

State legislatures throughout the country are slashing education funding as federal stimulus dollars expire and the public sector is finally feeling the full force of the recent recession. Opportunistic agenda-setters are attempting capitalize on antitaxation sentiment as financial troubles linger, encouraging legislatures to enact education funding rollbacks and broader privatization schemes (Underwood, 2011). As the state budget in Pennsylvania was finalized this summer, school districts in Allegheny County, which includes the city of Pittsburgh and 42 other school districts, announced teacher layoffs and furloughs and proposed other ways to cut spending, including consolidation of special education services, moving away from the trend toward mainstreaming students with special needs in their home schools

(Walck, 2011). Some districts are considering four-day weeks and cancelling their kindergarten programs (Niederberger, 2011). The latest financial difficulties come on top of increased competition for resources with charter schools and cyber schools. Like districts in many states, Pennsylvania districts face rising costs for health care and pension obligations, and they run up against local authorities unwilling or unable to raise millage rates to draw in more tax money.

Many states have already rushed to rewrite their school policies and labor laws to make themselves eligible for federal education dollars through the *Race for the Top* competitions, altering in unknown ways the landscape of educational practice. After the 2010 elections swept in majorities in many state legislatures intent on cutting taxes and public services, some politicians have successfully painted public workers as privileged, living off taxpayers while many private sector workers have lost their jobs or have had to settle for lower-paying jobs.

The *Race for the Top* reform agenda comes on top of ten years of schools and districts altering their practice in response to state accountability systems developed to comply with the federal *No Child Left Behind* legislation. Schools and districts have responded in varied ways, with the most changes coming in schools which are the target for accountability reform: so called "low-performing" schools, mostly those that serve a large number of children in poverty, many schools in urban school systems. Schools that are "well-positioned" to perform in state accountability systems have changed too, but not as drastically, at times placing greater emphasis on their students' test scores or devoting attention to "bubble kids," those who are most likely to score proficiently on standardized tests with greater attention. Sporadic cheating on tests has also been reported, with the revelations of systematic, coordinated cheating in the Atlanta Public Schools (Wilson, Bowers, & Hyde, 2011) to date the most extensive exposé of cheating. In some districts with higher test scores, the state proficiency standards are too low, so that schools pay only minimal attention to testing or the accountability system, except perhaps in relation to the performance of districts in their area that compete for prestige.

With the most recent shift to cutting back spending on public education and reducing collective bargaining for public school teachers, education policy continues its drift into structural manipulations to force changes in practices. Schools that are the target of accountability legislation are now left with fewer resources and more obligations. At the national level, the Obama administration's educational concerns have taken the form of tweaking *No Child Left Behind* and exploring neo-liberal concerns for greater competition and increased reliance on charter schools for innovation, all structural concerns without research support. The most lauded reformers of the past few years, Joel Klein in New York and Michelle Rhee in the District of Columbia, both heroes of educational improvement via high-stakes incentive strategies, are beginning to look less like miracle workers and more like short-term apple polishers. The New York City Public Schools' purported test score gains lost their luster when it was revealed that gains were largely due to declines over the years in the score the state of New York defined as "proficient" (Otterman & Gebeloff, 2010). As *USA Today* revealed (Gillum & Bello, 2011), the District of Columbia Public Schools' test results in 103 schools indicated inordinately large numbers of erasures, prompting an investigation of potential cheating. Rhee initially denied the veracity of the story but then acknowledged that widespread cheating was possible (Turque, 2011).

In such a volatile and varied context, what does it mean to be a professional in a public school? We are at a time in history when it is challenging to be a professional educator and to even think of oneself as a professional. Newspapers, magazines, and websites are flush with discussion about the problems of public education. The popular discourse about public education has for so long taken a bird's eye view, with policy makers taking a broad, national view (Ravitch [2010] refers to it as "seeing like a state" [p. 10]). In this book, I purposely do not start with a broad view. My approach is to focus more locally—on the actions of educators themselves who are struggling to act as professionals in settings every day. I offer a critique and a framework for responding. I refer to it as an active/ethical framework, "active" for an active philosophy of education for possibility and "ethical" for cultivating relations of responsibility.

I want this book to contribute substantively to the educational discourse. Much in the popular discourse of education is lacking in educational ideas—interesting methods of instruction, important concepts, invigorating experiences. Readers should not expect to come away from this book with new silver-bullet organizational schemes to try to fix the system. I want them to rethink their philosophies of education and professional ethics. My argument is not for a specific philosophy of education or ethics but for a new way to think about the importance of both, particularly now, after ten years of national high-stakes accountability policy has distorted the very language of public education and public educators face an uncertain economic future. I write for educators, educational leaders, and those preparing for those roles, with the hope of providing a framework for thinking differently that may lead to freer, more innovative and sustainable educational practices.

For this book, I draw from essays and conference papers that I have written and published elsewhere, pulling together the ideas into an extended engagement with the philosophical and ethical challenges of high-stakes accountability policy. The earlier work has been taken apart and put back together into a more cohesive whole. Most chapters are a combination of ideas from various pieces I've written, along with new ideas, frames, and examples drawn from subsequent reading, writing, and researching. Since 2004, I have collaborated with multiple colleagues on periodic interview studies with educators in Oklahoma and Pennsylvania on how high-stakes accountability policy interacts with their philosophies of education. Some selected examples from those studies are used here to help explain the context, my critiques of that context, and the articulation of the active/ethical framework that educators may use to respond.

In the preparation of this manuscript, I am grateful to many colleagues who have shaped my thinking. Stacy Otto, Andrea Hyde, and Noreen Garman read and commented on earlier drafts and provoked my thinking a number of times, and not just on this project. Numerous graduate students at the University of Pittsburgh, especially those who have come through the Doctoral Core in Administrative and Policy Studies over the last seven years, have been generous and patient with their reading and comments of earlier work on this topic, and Pitt colleagues Charlene Trovato, Maureen McClure, Maureen Porter, and Jerry Longo have at key points helped me see my way through this project. David Barker at Continuum Press got the ball rolling by inviting me to consider a book. My mentor, Lynda Stone, first introduced me to Michel Foucault and has encouraged this and all other projects in my academic career. I first became interested in accountability policy when it came into conflict with the North Carolina A+ Schools Program, which I studied under George Noblit's direction. I co-led a research team studying the Oklahoma A+ Schools with colleagues Diane Montgomery, Nancy Barry, and Michael Raiber. I collaborated with Cindy Gerstl-Pepin and Judie Mathers on two projects on accountability when I was at Oklahoma State, and both helped me to find my voice as a philosopher amid the policy discourse. At Oklahoma State, graduate students who worked on these various projects were Esia Anders, Jeanene Barnett, Belen Burkhalter, Shannon Goodsell, Dewayne Dickens, David Payne, and Bret Wood. A grant from the College of Education and Dean Ann Candler-Lotven supported data collection for this project. At Pitt, graduate students and graduates who worked on this project were Jillian Bichsel, Joshua Childs, Treva Clark, Marzia Cozzolino, Joseph Dietrich, Thomas Hallman, Andrea Hyde, Veronica Kozar, Julie Nagashima, Matt Rhodes, Gabriela Silvestre, and Dana Winters. Funding from the School of Education and Dean Alan Lesgold supported data collection and graduate student research support. A reading group at Pitt led by Julie Brooks and Ellen Motohashi helped me think through the theory and keep it all in perspective. Along the way, vital support and dialogue came from Pam Bettis, Elizabeth Bishop, Sue Books, Lisa Cary, Jenny Gordon, Daniel Narey, Robert Nash, Ryan Noel, Richard Quantz, and Virginia Worley. Educational reformers who greatly facilitated my understanding of this topic include Gerry Howell and Jean Hendrickson, as well as educators Gaye Weatherman and Leslie Clark. My work is possible and worthwhile because of my family, especially Deborah Desjardins and my boys, Joshua and Adam. Thank you all for contributing to this work.

Previously published material appears here with the permission of the original publishers.

Theory Into Practice published "High-Stakes Testing and the Default Philosophy of Education," in 2003 in Vol. 42, No. 1, and portions of that article appear in Chapters 2 and 8 with permission of the copyright holder, Taylor & Francis Ltd. (http://www.tandf.co.uk/journals).

Educational Studies published "Normalizing the Educated Subject: A Foucauldian Analysis of High-Stakes Testing," in 2006 in Vol. 39, No. 3. Sections of this article appear throughout the book, but mostly in Chapters 2, 5, and 6, with permission of Taylor & Francis Ltd., the copyright holder (http://wwwtandf.co.uk/journals).

Teachers College Record published "Care of the Self in a Context of Accountability," in 2008 in Vol. 110, No. 10 and at http://www.TCRecord.org. Teachers College holds the copyright and has granted permission for the article to reappear here. It forms portions of Chapters 5 and 6 and a small portion of Chapter 1.

Philosophical Studies in Education published "Resistance as a Component of Educator Professionalism," an earlier version of a portion of Chapter 7, in 2007 in Vol. 38 and at http://ovpes.org. The Ohio Valley Philosophy of Education Society sponsors the journal and has granted permission for the article's use in this publication.

1

The high-stakes accountability context

Jill after 25 years

Jill Bartoni is an Italian American high school English teacher who taught in the same Western Pennsylvania school district for 25 years. In January 2006, her last year of teaching at Hancock High School,[1] she spoke with a researcher from the University of Pittsburgh about her philosophy of education and how it had been affected by high-stakes accountability policy. Jill said that one of the reasons she was retiring at the end of the year was that she could no longer be complicit with educational practices that over time had become so test-driven that preparing for standardized tests was taken for granted as the school's purpose.

In Jill's view, the encroachment of standardized testing into education has been gradual over the years, culminating in the state accountability system that Pennsylvania put in place to comply with the *No Child Left Behind Act* (NCLB) (107th Congress, 2002). High-stakes accountability policy has put so much pressure on teachers and students, Jill believes, that the meaning and value of education has changed:

> For me, the testing has sucked the life out of—[*long pause*]. And I've been thinking a lot about this. My impression is that the spark to learn has been snuffed out, and I have been seeing this more and more over the last decades, as the testing has come more into play. I get students who are good students. I teach a lot of what we would call the upper-track students, and they are very academically aggressive. But they are very passive. The mentality is more and more, "Tell me what it is I have to do. Tell me how to do it. Tell me what I have to do to make the high score." It's really not about anything deeper or more profound. It's not making them life-long learners.

In her school, a rural high school in a small district well outside the city of Pittsburgh, students have performed well on the Pennsylvania 9th Grade Writing Assessment, and Jill for many years was responsible for preparing them for the writing assessment. She did a good job preparing them for the assessment, but she did not like giving up six weeks of the first quarter to prepare students for the assessment. Before coming to her, students were largely proficient, based on their eighth grade scores. As she put it: "I am not taking credit, since they had been indoctrinated all the way up. What I have been able to do with them is move them up from 'proficient' to 'advanced.'" Those scores mattered much to her school's standing in the state's accountability program, and her principal expected her to continue to do well: "It was a stressful time for me. . . . So the pressure was on, and even though I would talk to [the principal] about [how much] it would cost in terms of the overall curriculum, she wasn't interested."

In describing her philosophy of education, Jill says that education is about "what it means to live in the world, to know, to be an active citizen, to be an active participant, to make meaning." Later, she says that education is "a means of owning one's life in the world. That to me is where . . . freedom is embedded . . . freeing and liberating and opening possibilities." As an example of how she enacts her philosophy of education, Jill describes a reporting activity she has done with students to teach them the basic process of conducting research:

> I won't let them use the word report, I tell them it's research and that they are researchers . . . and that I don't want them to see themselves as reporters but as researchers. And so we talk about the difference between what it means to report instead of research something. And I guess I'm finding that my own academic background is making my teaching harder instead of easier.

As Jill mentions in this passage, she wants her students to know how to do research and to become stronger thinkers. Her challenge is to get the students to think past the report they need to submit for a grade, to become interested in a topic that is important to them, to locate an important issue in the topic, and to learn how to pose questions. Interestingly, she expresses the value of the assignment as building in them an understanding of who they are *becoming*, researchers rather than reporters, the implication being that as they become stronger questioners, they will become something new. To put it differently, Jill provides them opportunities to cultivate themselves, to imagine what they can be, and to care for the ways in which they are becoming more. In her words, she wants them to take charge of their own education.

That is not the philosophy of education that she sees being encouraged in her school. Arguing that "so much of what good teachers do with students in the course of a day is very difficult to measure," Jill is concerned that teachers are discouraged from becoming better teachers, and many of the younger teachers are unaware of how much things have changed and are willing to comply with instrumental teaching and learning.

Increased emphasis on testing has made school "what we do to do something else," Jill says, preparing students to get good grades and to do well on tests so that they can excel later on. She argues that testing has altered what counts as knowledge in school and how that affects parents and teachers:

> The tests themselves make a certain kind of learning or knowledge legitimate, because the powers that be make that claim. So they have the authority. The tests have the authority. And the parents trust the tests and the test maker, who are not us. . . . And we then just become the public servants who are paid by the district to teach to those tests.

Jill is frustrated that tests have become an authority more powerful than teachers in determining how well students are succeeding. Tests seem to have reversed places with teachers, to put it differently. They determine curriculum and instruction.

Uncomfortable with her own place in taking for granted the power of testing, Jill finds herself questioning how it has changed her at times:

> Sometimes I feel it's really almost unethical. Complicit. Complicit with the forces that I'm opposed to, when I find myself taking 6 weeks, doing it well, having them be successful. They want it. Their parents want it. My part in it is—it turns into really an ethical dilemma for me, and it's counter to the pedagogy that has evolved in my life and what it means to be a teacher.

Jill has continued to teach from her philosophy of education and to focus on giving students the opportunity to grow as thinkers and researchers. Trying to change the system, as the system has tried to change her, has been largely futile. She has participated in district meetings for picking textbooks; over time choices became limited to the textbook companies that have aligned their textbooks with the state standards. Talking to her principal about her misgivings was futile. The principal held monthly faculty meetings to discuss student test scores and to develop interventions to help more students become proficient. The principal held the meetings because the state required her to do so. Teachers eventually became very frustrated with these meetings, because it seemed that none of their ideas for helping students were ever put into place. Similarly, students scoring below basic on tests were required to attend sessions for special assistance, but they were not actually receiving any help during those sessions; the principal organized supervised study halls with instruction so that the school would be in compliance.

> Some of us have discussed this and we use the word impotent. We feel impotent. On the other hand, there is anger for us, and I feel that I can speak for them too. There is anger that can infect [us]. It can find [its] way into our teaching, and we try to find a way to keep it out of the classroom, but it comes out in the meetings. The anger at the after school meetings is very explosive.

Engaging with parents is another possible way to try to change the school, but Jill finds them to be just as focused as the principal on test scores. She explains with empathy how she believes parents have come to attribute meaning to test scores:

> Parents, by and large, want what's best for their children. Many of them are in the same place as some of us who teach. They want their children to do well, and if tests become the way to measure the value of success and they are the only way, then I think they see me and [the other] teachers— that if we are doing our jobs, then their children should be scoring well.

Here Jill shows how parents come to expect their children's teachers to provide them with educational services that result in a desired outcome— scoring well.

Perhaps the one story Jill told that was most bothersome to her about her experience at her school is a reference to a practice that elsewhere has come to be called the "bubble kids" phenomenon:

> I will tell you this for a fact, and I would hope that this would make this somewhere into your study. I was told this directly from my principal: "Do not worry about the students who are below basic. I'm not concerned about them. I want you to work with the basic students to move them to proficiency, because that's where we have the best shot of upping our scores." I sat there that day and I thought, "How can I be a party to this?" And I'm sure that all of this plays into my decision to retire this year.

Jill's principal is focused on the school maximizing the number of children who can score as "proficient" or "advanced" on standardized tests. Jill notes that the principal made this statement publicly and without irony:

> What shocked me about her statement is that she made it in a public arena. . . . It sounded as if it was a given. It was, "Well, you should feel that way too" . . . . We do the job, then she looks good, then we can be on the list. . . . I've stopped caring about those things—that if you are put on

the list twice, then the Big Bad Wolf is going to come in to take over, all that scary stuff. We're supposed to be afraid.

Jill does mention fear again. She is not only concerned for herself and her students but also the implications of this practice for public education:

I'm scared about the future of public education, about moves to privatize it, I'm scared about a generation of students coming out who don't know how to read between the lines, don't know how to question. It's a culture of fear. Everybody is fearful. Fear grips people, and so in the grip of that fear, you act.

Being active and ethical while under surveillance

Jill Bartoni is an educator facing the day-to-day challenges of high-stakes accountability policy in public schools. In this summary, taken from an interview conducted in January 2006, Jill names the real dangers associated with an accountability policy that attaches high stakes to standardized testing. States are required by federal law to develop accountability systems that apply rewards and sanctions to encourage schools to increase the number of students (overall and in key subgroups) who can become proficient in tested areas of the curriculum. Districts are encouraged by state policy to align their curricula and instructional strategies to state standards and the state testing program. Principals are encouraged to enact policies to raise proficiency levels. Teachers are encouraged to enact practices that conform to the policies laid before them. As Jill shows, many of those policies and practices come up against teachers' philosophies of education and their ethical standards.

This book is about what it means to be active and ethical while under the surveillance of high-stakes accountability policy. I begin each of the first seven chapters with stories from schools under pressure from state accountability systems. The various schools, districts, and states I draw from vary in how they are faring in relation to accountability pressures. In some cases, the effect is much less pronounced than in the case of Jill's school, but educators I have encountered over the last 16 years agree that some effects can be found in any public school. All over the United States (and in several other countries, like Australia and the United Kingdom, who have adopted similar accountability policies), educators like Jill Bartoni face pressure from state accountability systems, whether or not they are under threat of some sort of sanction. What makes being an educator particularly challenging in the current era is that the pressures are not always direct; instead they infuse educational practice. One of the most compelling and surprising indications, as Jill describes, is when teachers, principals, and parents seem to take the pressure for granted—proceeding without questioning, changing their practice, falling in line, and as later stories suggest, without even being asked to fall in line.

With one exception, the stories come from research studies I have conducted as a faculty member or participated in as a graduate student, starting in 1995, when I joined a collaborative research team studying the North Carolina A+ Schools Program, now the N.C. A+ Schools Network, a group of K-12 public schools adopting a whole-school reform model based on arts integration. Additional stories come from the Oklahoma A+ Schools, a second network of schools based on the model of the North Carolina program and whose research and evaluation team I codirected while a faculty member at Oklahoma State University. A third source of stories is from an extended study of the effects of high-stakes accountability policy on educators' philosophies of education, begun and codirected in Oklahoma in January 2004 and then continuing to 2011 in Pennsylvania, where I have been a faculty member at the University of Pittsburgh since September 2004. This book is not a comprehensive analysis of any of these studies, but instead a philosophical critique and argument for an alternative framework that makes use of stories from the various studies to give examples. More detailed information about these studies can be found in the Appendix to this volume.

I begin with Jill's story because in one short interview, Jill provides multiple glimpses in just one school of many of the dangerous exercises of power that proliferate under high-stakes accountability. Michel Foucault (1995/1975) would refer to these as examples of how surveillance works to discipline docile subjects into exercising power over themselves, a seemingly mundane exercise of power that he argues is nevertheless the most effective form of discipline in the modern age. I am interested in all of these exercises of power that proliferate in response to high-stakes accountability policy. I am mostly interested in how educators talk about their practice in relation to these exercises of power, what happens to their philosophies of education, and what it all means ethically. I am interested in this key problem: *how high-stakes accountability policy proliferates educational practices that displace philosophies of education and professional ethics.*

My concern is that accountability policy has had the ironic effect of making teachers, principals, and schools less responsible for students' educational progress, because it has destabilized educators' own notions of professionalism. I aim over the course of the book to depict these problems and issues as philosophical problems, questions that require us as educators to rethink fundamentally the meaning and value that we ascribe to education. I argue that without attention fundamentally to the ethical practice of educators as professionals, we're not likely to improve the situation. By attaching high stakes to standardized test scores, accountability policy has effected what Foucault refers to as a reversal of power relations: a test score that was designed to be one measure (among many) of educational achievement, to be one small tool to help gauge progress, has become the goal. Through exercises of power on a grand scale (in terms of policy) and, perhaps more importantly, on a day-to-day basis (in terms of practices and decisions that educators and administrators make about what, how, and who to teach), educators have supplanted the meaning and value of education for the sake of "student achievement," as determined by standardized testing.

In this book, I build a critique of the everyday effects of high-stakes accountability policy and offer a framework for how educators may respond through a renewed sense of professionalism. I aim to use the tools of philosophy to construct a series of arguments about the problems of public education and to offer potential solutions, not in terms of policy, for that is beyond the scope of this book, but for the professional practice of teachers, principals, and other administrators.

To focus on philosophies of education and professional ethics, I am interested in the ethics of the everyday—how we treat each other on a day-to-day basis in public schools, how we decide to act in response to explicit and implicit pressure of high-stakes accountability policy, and how we protect what we believe to be the meaning and value of education. Following the theory of disciplinary power of Foucault, I explain the subtle workings of power that proliferate *normalization*—the establishment of a norm from which all others are judged and disciplined—through the technology of the examination. A danger associated with the use of standardized testing, normalization is a conceptual problem that I explain in detail in Chapter 5. It is evident as an underlying problem in several strata of high-stakes accountability. It is evident in the rhetoric of accountability policy, conflating accountability for scores with responsibility for children, a problem I address in Chapter 2. It plays out in the specific systems that states created to comply with NCLB, the policies that districts put into place to succeed in their state systems, and within school buildings, the actions of school leaders, teachers, and students (and as Jill's story makes clear, the actions of parents). As educators, we need to draw attention to these phenomena and understand normalization's reach so that we can articulate alternatives for ourselves and our students. We need robust philosophies of education and professional ethics, strong enough to account for, work through, disrupt, and resist normalizing power relations.

To respond to the dangers of normalization, I offer a two-part framework for responsible educators—the active and the ethical—that work together to resist the dangers associated with high-stakes accountability policy. The framework is not a cookbook or a guidebook for educators, but instead a way of thinking differently about one's professional practice. The "active" part is a call for educators to actively develop and assert a philosophy of education based on possibility (rather than normalization, which I argue needs to be resisted). In order to facilitate possibility, the "ethical" part is a call for educators to cultivate relations of responsibility (rather than accountability, which has become a distortion of responsibility). The relations of responsibility are intrapersonal (the responsibility an educator has toward herself or himself), relational (responsibilities toward proximal others), and public (responsibilities educators have toward all others).

Foucault provides the conceptual framework for the critique as well as much of the responding framework. Foucault is the French social theorist who early on in his intellectual career articulated a structuralist position on the changing character of knowledge across time (an archaeology of knowledge) and later developed a post-structural position on the development of the modern self. He then in the last years of his life articulated an ethic based on the Ancient Greek notion of the care of the self. In education, Foucault is most well known for his critiques of disciplinary power, most notably in *Discipline and Punish: The Birth of the Prison* (1995/1975), which has been applied to analyses of power relations in schools. Late in his life, Foucault built upon historical critique of the modern self and the exploration of hidden possibilities through cultivation of an ethics that appears to be quite different from ethics as typically described in the modern Western tradition. As I show later on, Foucault's ethics fits Jill's example well, because it highlights the importance of two "projects" that Jill undertakes as a teacher. First, she enacts a role for herself as a teacher who is vigilant to dangerous ways in which she exercises power over her students (subjecting them to a six-week regimen of test preparation that serves to a significant extent the purpose of keeping her school away from the Big Bad Wolf). Second, she enacts a philosophy of education that encourages her students to become better thinkers so that they may open up additional educational possibilities for themselves and also, perhaps more importantly, to take charge of their own education.

As Jill's example shows, teachers are in the double-bind position of being both normalized and normalizing, the technology of the examination being the central feature in the power relations that serve to normalize. This is a very difficult position in which to find oneself. Evoking the metaphor of the panopticon (Foucault, 1995/1975), educators both exercise surveillance over students and sit in a position of being under surveillance. Consistent with the panopticon, educators are not entirely cognizant of the ways in which surveillance works on those for whom they are responsible, nor are they always aware of the ways in which they are anonymously under surveillance.

The norm upon which the technology of the examination is based takes on outsized proportions, effecting the reversal of power relations I mention above (Foucault, 1995/1975). This power dynamic privileges a nonreflective philosophy of education by default and circumscribes discourse about educational philosophies and practices in classrooms, schools, districts, and state departments of education. A "default" philosophy of education is my term for the philosophy of education that results from a lack of reflective, engaged dialogue by educators and school communities about their goals and practice (Gunzenhauser, 2003). One default philosophy in our current context of schooling is one that places inordinate value on the scores achieved on high-stakes tests, rather than on the achievement that the scores are supposed to represent. A "default" philosophy of education takes precedence over the substantial work that teachers and school communities need to do daily to create their own philosophies of education.

The default philosophy underlying high-stakes testing is a philosophy of education in which tests designed to be part of a system of accountability drive the curriculum, limit instructional innovation, and keep educators from establishing for themselves their priorities and visions of what education should be. Because of the high stakes attached to the tests, policy has had the unintended effect of encouraging a "default" philosophy of education: a vision of education that values highly what can be measured, and more problematically, it values most highly the measurement itself. When this "default" philosophy of education dominates, other possible philosophies of education are more difficult both to articulate and to implement. That is probably the most unfortunate aspect of high-stakes testing, because conversations in communities about the meaning and value of education cannot take place without performance on standardized tests taking center stage. Most fundamentally, these dangerous aspects of high-stakes accountability policy present a crisis of the educated self, because they authorize practices and conditions that constrain opportunities for educators and students to constitute themselves.

Pressures to meet the demands for external accountability create conditions in which the normalized and normalizing roles can overtake an educator who does not have a rather complicated sense of herself or himself as an actor in relation to others. Jill is an uncommon example of an educator who can critique her situation; however, the conditions under which she worked in her school district made it difficult for her to continue resisting normalization when she had the opportunity to retire. Educators without her critical capabilities who experience similar conditions may find it very difficult to comprehend the scope of the issues they face and may find it that much more difficult to care for themselves, much less to participate in relations that contribute to the care of self in others.

To be ethical, educators not only need to resolve ethical dilemmas in defensible ways, but they also need to recognize themselves as powerful in relation to others. To be active, educators need to be vigilant for moments when they are placed in the position to be "reactive" to normalizing pressures, and they also need to develop clear notions of how they may create opportunities for the cultivation of educational selves—selves that are rich ethically, aesthetically, epistemologically, and politically. With the active and ethical notions taken together, the active/ethical professional is a grounded educator who is able to resist unreasonable demands placed upon him or her, to protect students from the worst of the normalizing pressures of accountability, and to create educational systems and structures that work against normalization.

In studying the effects of accountability policy on education for the past ten years, I have at times thought of philosophy of education as endangered of extinction. I want to be clear at the outset that philosophy of education does not provide all the answers. However, passionate, committed and experienced educators may use philosophy of education in very important ways, essentially to reorient themselves to their selves (questionable syntax but that is what I mean), to their practice, and perhaps most importantly, to others. I am confident, for instance, in the abilities of my graduate students in the School of Education at the University of Pittsburgh to innovate expansively, based upon their critical engagement with their professional practice, their moral commitments, and their rich educational ideas. Educational ideas are almost completely absent from the current discourse about accountability and how to fix it moving forward. For my graduate students and others like them, I wish to convey the conceptual power of Foucauldian ethics in a manner that is useful for understanding their practice with appropriate complexity and with an eye toward educational possibilities. I want readers to gain a sense of ways in which they might refocus their educational efforts on improving their practice as an ethical endeavor, one that helps them and their students to constitute themselves in ways that expand rather than constrain possibilities. I also want them to feel comfortable engaging ethical theory and to see it as directly relevant to their professional practice.

Although the book draws from some work previously published, I have designed the book with its own comprehensive argument about what professionalism may look like as we as educators continue to struggle with the challenges of high-stakes accountability policy and whatever comes next. In Chapter 2, I go into greater detail about how accountability policy leads to philosophical problems for educators, from the conceptual conflation of responsibility and accountability to the default philosophy of education and problematic professional ethics. Chapter 3 situates my work in the ethical traditions of philosophy and related ethics work in education. In Chapter 4, I focus on the importance of "relation" as a concept for responding to accountability pressures. After that are chapters that bring in Foucault's theories of discipline, ethics, and resistance, addressed respectively in Chapter 5, Chapter 6, and Chapter 7. Chapter 7 is also where I begin to explain the active/ethical framework in more detail. Chapter 7 provides the conceptual basis for the framework, and Chapter 8 revisits the examples throughout the text to provide examples of active/ethical professionalism in practice.

Note

1 Jill Bartoni and Hancock High School are pseudonyms for an interview participant and her employer. Except when specifically noted otherwise, all educator and school names are pseudonyms for participants from research studies in which the author participated from 1995 to 2011. The research studies are explained in greater detail in the Appendix.

2

Accountability as a philosophical problem

The success of Jess

Many years ago, just as the state of Oklahoma was developing an accountability system that would comply with the strictures of NCLB, I had a conversation with Debbie Bendick, who at the time was a middle-school principal and a doctoral student developing an idea for her dissertation (Bendick, 2003). In her school, located in an affluent suburban school district, the children's test scores were among the highest in the state. Statewide publications at the time were already publishing lists of the schools in the state with the top Academic Performance Index (API) scores.

For her dissertation, Debbie was interested in conducting a case study of another school, also in her school district, which had even higher test scores and an even higher ranking in the newspaper than her school. Based on what Debbie knew of the principal at that school, her colleague Jess Edison, she suspected that he understood something about cultivating relationships in his building, and she was intent on learning from a systematic case study of his practice. In our conversation, she provided multiple rationales for why cultivating relationships could be important for effective school leadership, including references from the research literature. She suggested various forms of evidence of the effects his approach to cultivating relationships was having on Jess' school. For example, as she describes in her dissertation, at Jess' school, teachers use family metaphors to describe the community feel of the school, and Jess cultivates a community of memory in the school (Sergiovanni, 1994) that links teachers and students across generations.

However, when we had our initial conversation about her interest in Jess' school, Debbie discounted all of the substantive evidence of success in light of what she saw as the ultimate indicator: the student test scores. And while she agreed with the caveat that test scores are a proxy for student achievement—one kind of indicator of student success, with a built-in margin of error, and built-in caveats that the tests were not designed to measure the quality of a school—she did not disentangle herself from the belief that those test scores were the ultimate arbiter of quality and that they must mean that he was doing a better job than she was. This belief subtly made its way into the beginning pages of her dissertation:

> But who is to say that relationships, initiated and nurtured by a principal, are not what will get a building to those results—test results and all other data that suggest a school has an undeniable potential for building and increasing its capacity. (Bendick, 2003, p. 4)

After this early statement, Debbie then sets aside the test scores to tell the story of the school and its principal and how it meets Sergiovanni's definition of a school community and further meets Noddings' (1992) definition of a caring community. As Debbie describes in detail, cultivating supportive working relationships among educational staff can foster a community of caring and supportive pedagogical relationships with students. She makes this conclusion about her colleague Jess:

> He has consciously worked to create a culture of caring, created one relationship at a time, to build a strong foundation that would support the professional and personal growth of each member of the staff. . . . While other outside factors which cannot be mitigated from within the school walls may affect the rate at which any single teacher can evolve and mature, the setting within the school provides a best case scenario for each teacher's success. One teacher at a time and many teachers together, most operating from a perspective of personal duty to the good of the community, they create . . . continuous capacity building. (p. 157)

The rarity of philosophizing for educational practice

My conversation with Debbie was the first time I suspected that something powerful was happening as a result of high-stakes accountability policy. As states in 2002 and 2003 were in the process of developing their accountability systems to comply with NCLB, I was curious about the power that standardized testing already had on the ways in which educators talked about their educational practice and what they believed to be the meaning and value of education. Debbie's presumption of the authority of standardized test score data as an indicator of school quality was an important power dynamic that repeated itself. In graduate classes, at meetings, and during research interviews, I came across educators continually who would identify interesting educational ideas, but then discount their value in deference to measurable effects on standardized test scores.

In my work as a university faculty member and educational philosopher and qualitative researcher for the last 12 years, I have found that the language of philosophy of education is rarely used by teachers and school leaders to describe their visions or the challenges they face to be externally accountable. Every once in a while, however, an individual educator or group of educators will come together around an intriguing educational idea, which may help them rethink their practice, to open up a possibility that had been heretofore unknown to them. These indeed are the moments that one lives for as an educator and researcher. At other times, students articulate their struggles and then identify their responses: sometimes numbing or painful acquiescence, but other times principled resistance to imposed barriers. And even more intriguingly, they may share an example of a form of resistance that most people wouldn't recognize as resistance, or even struggle, but is resistance all the same, because it creates an opening for a new possibility—a reframing, a rethinking, a reconstituting of role, a reconstituting of self.

More often, it has been important for me to understand the compromises they have made and to understand with empathy, so that together we might name what has occurred and begin to envision alternatives. In the extant literature about accountability's effect on educators, there is an underlying sense in which the professions of PreK-12 education are being de-skilled and de-professionalized in the service of higher test scores. Concerns include the ethical dilemmas associated with test preparation (Mathison & Freeman, 2003), wherein teachers are finding they have to choose between curriculum and instruction that they believe to be educative and that they believe students need to perform well on tests.

In this chapter, I describe the various issues that have arisen from high-stakes accountability policy and highlight the conceptual philosophical problems that play out as real and troubling issues for educators.

Documented effects of accountability policy

In this section I synthesize the literature on the effects of high-stakes accountability policy, drawing from research conducted at various times in the accountability era, including research in states whose accountability systems predate NCLB (and informed features of the national legislation) and research that has focused on the effects of NCLB.

In his review of the literature several years ago, Sirotnik (2004) noted the appearance "nearly every month ... [of] new studies documenting the failure of high-stakes testing ... and some studies still trying to find the pony in the manure pile" (p. 7). The research on the effects of accountability policy has followed the emergence of the standards movement and the celebrated successes of several states' accountability programs, both developments emerging prior to the dramatic reorganization of the federal role in education through the NCLB legislation. Many of the initial commentators on this phenomenon were policy researchers and advocates of high standards, who debated the efficacy of external standards, rewards, and sanctions (Carnoy et al., 2003; Elmore & Fuhrman, 2001; Skrla & Scheurich, 2004). The phenomenon also drew the attention of researchers who noticed the impact that high-stakes accountability was having on other school reforms that they had been studying already, such as arts integration and inquiry learning (Gunzenhauser & Gerstl-Pepin, 2002; Jorgenson & Vanosdall, 2002) and on nontested areas of the curriculum (Jones et al., 2003).

Several years after the NCLB legislation, large-scale studies took account of the effectiveness of the national policy. The RAND Corporation has produced multiple reports on how the legislation has affected state education policies, school and district practices, and teacher and school leader attitudes. The RAND study results are synthesized for policy makers in an extensive report (Stecher et al., 2010), which also provides recommendations on what policy makers need to do to implement the policy more effectively in the future. Two RAND reports summarize school changes during the period 2004 to 2006 in California, Georgia, and Pennsylvania from a project called Implementing Standards-Based Accountability (ISBA) (Hamilton et al., 2007; Stecher et al., 2008).

In the ISBA study, researchers assessed how well the NCLB policy succeeded with its goals, how correct policy makers were with their assumptions about teacher behaviors, and how it was changing practice in relation to the stated policy goals for math and science; the reports do not investigate the soundness of the policy itself or the effect on other areas of the curriculum. Notable for its extensive data collection, mixed methods, and multi-year data collection, the study involved educators at various levels, parents, and some students. It is characterized by large-scale quantitative research and small-scale mixed methods case studies. Unlike many studies of accountability, the precision of this research helps document changing attitudes and practices upon which a philosophical analysis can be based.

Also helpful is another large-scale study, conducted by the Harvard Civil Rights Project, which took a different approach, investigating the effects of the policy to analyze whether or not high-stakes accountability is a policy that should continue (Sunderman et al., 2005). This study was conducted in six states (Arizona, California, Georgia, Illinois, New York, and Virginia), and although its data is very similar to the RAND study, calling the desirability of accountability policy into question leads to dramatically different interpretations, implications, and suggestions for policy improvement.

What have states done?

I begin this synthesis by focusing on what states have done as the entities responsible for creating high-stakes accountability systems. While some states had accountability systems in place well before NCLB, most did not, so in most cases, states developed accountability systems to comply with federal law, not of their own initiative. As a result, many states have acted to comply with the federal regulations, although several states initially considered foregoing federal education dollars so that they could retain control over how they govern their schools. The evidence suggests that states for the most part engineered their systems to comply with the law and to delay as much as possible the most questioned aspect of NCLB— the requirement that by 2014, 100 percent of students reach proficiency, including special education students on an Individual Education Plan (IEP). Other evidence suggests that states have redefined proficiency at such low levels over the years, that the measurements of proficiency lack coherent meaning. There is little evidence that states have built the capacity of schools to improve the educational experiences of all children or that any of their actions have the potential to build capacity or raise standards. Although there is some evidence that the strategy of rewards and sanctions has brought greater public attention to the specific places where achievement is low and resources are inequitable, there is little evidence that this attention has led to significant improvement.

Compliance

NCLB set the requirement of 100 percent proficiency by 2014, and states had the freedom to set proficiency goals for the intervening years. In the three states RAND studied, proficiency goals were graduated, with modest requirements in proficiency growth in the initial years and the last years requiring steeply improved proficiency, rising steadily in the final years to reach 100 percent proficiency in 2014 (Hamilton et al., 2007). In 2007, the Pennsylvania state secretary of education presented Pennsylvania's yearly proficiency requirements in a graph to a room full of faculty of educational leadership programs across the state, and he made a point of emphasizing that he believed that these goals were achievable. School leadership faculty did not believe these goals were obtainable, and neither did the sample of school leaders that RAND researchers surveyed. While majorities in the RAND study believed that they would reach Adequate Yearly Progress (AYP) the following year, only one in three "believed that their districts could attain their AYP targets for the next five years" (Hamilton et al., 2007, p. 49).

And as I mentioned in the Preface, in 2011, the US Secretary of Education, Arne Duncan, indicated that the proficiency goals of NCLB were now so unrealistic that as many as 80 percent of the schools would be named as low-performing in Fall 2011 unless Congress changed the law (Dillon, 2011). Research suggests that state-level improvements in achievement are limited to state tests and do not translate to the more general scores on the National Assessment for Educational Progress (NAEP), which Lee (2006) found to be modestly rising in math and remaining flat in reading at the same rate before and after NCLB:

> Consequently, continuation of the current trend will leave the nation far behind the NCLB target of 100 percent proficiency by 2014. Only 24 to 34 percent of students will meet the NAEP proficiency target in reading [with] 29 to 64 percent meeting that math proficiency target by 2014. (p. 11)

Ravitch (2010) interprets such modest progress on the NAEP as evidence that NCLB has failed, and she argues that, with the exception of Massachusetts, states have chosen to comply with the strictures of the law, rather than raising standards and holding schools accountable for higher standards.

Inadequate funding

According to school leaders in the RAND study, the biggest hindrance to the implementation of NCLB was funding. Nearly every superintendent said they lacked adequate funding to implement NCLB (Hamilton et al., 2007). According to the Harvard study, one of the reasons for that perspective may have been that embedded in the law were resources for only the first year, and subsequently, large amounts went to pay for private tutoring and other supplemental services and school choice costs (Sunderman et al., 2005). The funding, in other words, went to sources other than the school itself, so although funding may have benefitted school test scores, the ways in which funds were disbursed actually constrained the ability of schools to use funds for developing their capacity.

Inadequate accountability systems

As accountability policies have unfolded, some researchers have addressed ways in which the state accountability systems might be structured to more efficiently or more effectively reach the policy goals of NCLB. Other researchers have pointed out errors in the assumptions that policy makers have made about the match between specific tests and the ways in which they are used. There have been multiple ways proposed to fix accountability systems. For example, some educational evaluators advocate the use of assessments as part of accountability systems that integrate appropriate respect for the fallibility of educational measurements (American Evaluation Association, 2002; Linn, 2000; Mathison & Freeman, 2003; Rogers, 2005). Some advocates of high standards argue that high stakes should not be attached to tests, but otherwise that high standards, along with alternative forms of accountability, are appropriate bases and motivators for educational reform (Carnoy et al., 2003; Thompson, 2001). The standards-based reform movement existed prior to the advent of NCLB, and its advocates have continued to argue for its potential as a significant route to school improvement, if the problems with high-stakes accountability can be solved (Porter et al., 2004; Ravitch, 2010; Resnick & Zurawsky, 2005). It is important to distinguish between the establishment of educational standards, which some states had in place prior to NCLB, and the establishment of high-stakes accountability systems. These two related but distinct efforts at reform are quite often conflated, not unexpectedly since in many contexts, they appeared for the first time together. Scott Thompson (2001) distinguishes the two as authentic standards and high stakes testing, the latter being the "evil twin."

Others argue for systemic accountability, wherein policy makers and the public are made accountable for educational conditions (Oakes et al., 2004) and accountability systems themselves are evaluated not on their ability to force test scores to go up but on their efficacy in producing other meaningful educational outcomes (Sirotnik, 2004). Hamilton et al. (2007) conclude that states have not sufficiently explored more appropriate methods for measuring school and student performance, and Ravitch (2010) concludes that with the exception of Massachusetts, states have not only inappropriate but damaging testing systems in place. Ravitch and the RAND researchers recommend using smarter tests and policies that disable states from making the various compromises states have been allowed to make.

Low performance brought to light

There is also evidence that as a result of state accountability systems, the low performance of some schools has been brought to light in a manner that had not been as publicly clear before. While we might argue that at least attention is focusing on the low performance of some schools, there is only sporadic evidence that that attention has led to school improvement. A Texas study looked at one possible effect of bringing low performance to light—that it may motivate schools to learn more about the needs of children not performing well on testing and change practices to more culturally appropriate methods (Skrla & Scheurich, 2001, 2004; Skrla et al., 2000). Skrla and Scheurich sought out four schools in Texas that used the opportunity of high-stakes accountability to challenge their own deficit thinking, or in other words, the idea that students who perform poorly on measures of achievement do so partly because they lack abilities or experiences. A large body of research suggests countering deficit thinking by building on the strengths of students (strengths which may not be recognized without changing conventional approaches to schooling) to increase achievement (Valencia, 1997). Culturally responsive approaches to education have an increasing research base (see Baker & Digiovanni, 2005, for another approach to how culturally relevant pedagogy relates to standardization). Faced with the public availability of test scores not only of the whole district but of racial and socioeconomic groups, educators in the four districts in the Texas study addressed the gap in achievement scores between white and nonwhite students (Skrla & Scheurich, 2001, 2004). These districts were difficult for the researchers to identify, however, suggesting that the phenomenon was not widespread in Texas under its accountability system (Gunzenhauser & Hyde, 2007).

Special education and English-language learning

Perhaps the most curious aspect of NCLB is the insistence that all students be brought to proficiency by 2014. As NCLB continues, teachers question the appropriateness of NCLB mandates for all students to test as proficient, especially the students who qualify for special education services or who are learning the English language as a second language (English-language learning, or ELL). In their case study interviews, Hamilton et al. (2007) got a closer look at how this requirement interacted with accountability:

> Even the case study schools that felt they had done well with their ELL students expressed discontent with the way NCLB deals with ELLs. They felt that their progress with ELL students was not being recognized, since students who can pass the test are no longer designated as language learners. (p. 125)

While states have developed various methods for schools to exempt some students from testing, the policy still insists on the testing of students whose IEPs are purposely not aligned with grade-level standards. It is troubling enough that students have to be tested on material in which they are not being instructed; educators can deal with the absurdity and are skilled enough to mitigate discomfort students experience. When high stakes are attached to students' performance on these tests, a new set of conditions are created. In the next section, I explore how that phenomenon has played out for schools and for teachers.

What happens in schools?

In an accountability system, the primary unit of responsibility for student achievement is the school. High-stakes accountability policy builds on the logic that rewards and sanctions will motivate schools to meet high standards. Evidence from earlier state accountability systems suggested that rewards and sanctions were effective at changing school practices, especially at schools targeted for improvement, but not necessarily in the ways intended by the policy. Sanctions especially were shown to be effective for raising test scores, but not for increasing capacity (Carnoy et al., 2003). In their assessment of accountability systems that preceded NCLB, Elmore and Fuhrman (2001) proposed that in order to use assessments effectively, schools need internal accountability first, and by that they mean developing answers to fundamental aspects of accountability: "what they expect of students academically, what constitutes good instructional practice, who is responsible for student learning, and how individual students and teachers account for their work and learning" (p. 69). Elmore and Fuhrman found that in most schools under the gun of high-stakes testing, teachers were working harder, spending more time, and exerting more effort preparing students for testing. However, schools were not fundamentally improving what they were doing; instead they were devoting inordinate time concerned about students' scores and not enough about students' learning (Elmore & Fuhrman, 2001). After studying data from states after NCLB, Hamilton et al. (2007) reaffirm that appraisal, arguing that teacher and administrator capacity for improvement still needs to be developed.

Rewards and sanctions

In surveys of teachers in Colorado and Oklahoma, Judie Mathers (2004; see also King & Mathers, 1997) early on in the accountability movement found that teachers and principals already felt substantially responsible for student learning prior to the onset of high-stakes accountability programs, and teachers believed that neither rewards nor sanctions were likely to change their notions about to whom they felt accountable. However, they thought that the rewards and sanctions might change their practice. These insights have played out in the subsequent, larger scale work by Hamilton et al. (2007) and Sunderman et al. (2005). The logic of rewards and sanctions seems to be a poor match for schools. Noddings (2007) questions: "before imposing a set of threats, sanctions, and punishments on everyone, policy makers should have asked if a blame-and-punish approach is the best way to motivate people" (p. 34). Prior to NCLB, there was not sufficient research to support the idea that either sanctions or rewards motivate desirable changes in school policies or practices. Subsequently, there is little support for the idea that schools forced to change through rewards and sanctions become better schools. Oakes et al. (2004) suggest it is an issue of lacking knowledge and capacity: schools lacking the knowledge and capacity to improve are not likely to become better schools when forced to produce better scores.

Labeling

There have been documented effects on what it means for schools to be labeled through high-stakes accountability systems. Most effects have been associated with the "low-performing" label. By design, the label is supposed to hold accountable the professional staff associated with the school and communicate to parents which schools need improvement. Labeling can be especially problematic when subgroups within a school are the source of the stigmatic label. Smith and her associates (2004) found that within schools, conflicts may arise between different constituencies of parents when resources need to be shared or different groups need to share the same label because of the performance of one group. On a larger scale, Hamilton et al. (2007) found similar phenomena across the states they studied in relation to children who form a ELL subgroup: "when they are a subgroup that is seen to cause the school to fail to meet AYP, parents of local children begin to put pressure on the principal to find a way to exclude the ELLs from the school" (p. 125). The impulse to exclude low-scoring others should not be surprising, considering the fairly consistent and well-documented self-segregation that high-status parents seek for their children in public schools, whether by school or district.

In another unexpected twist, Hamilton et al. (2007) found recurring examples of administrators hiding from school personnel why the school had not done better on accountability measures, explaining away poor performance by nonexistent technical matters, perhaps in an effort to avoid school personnel having to internalize the low-performing label:

> In our case study visits, we encountered a number of teachers in schools or districts that had failed to make AYP, usually for the first time, who were misinformed about the reasons that the school or district had failed to make AYP. In these cases, it seemed like the principal or district administration had intentionally downplayed the results, focusing the blame on technicalities that they did not describe clearly to teachers. It appeared that this was the result of an attempt to keep up school morale and help the school community get past the stigma of failing. (p. 49)

The implication here is that the low-performing label is worse than the performance itself. This last phenomenon is a reversal of the logic of rewards and sanctions—the sanction, which is supposed to motivate school personnel to improve their practice, is reconstituted as a technical problem so that teachers don't even realize the need to improve their practice.

High standards

One of the chief rationales for high-stakes accountability policy is that it is a method for raising standards and holding all children to the same high standard. On the effectiveness of this goal, there is mixed evidence. It appears that educators in the states that RAND studied believed that high-stakes accountability policy led to greater academic rigor in the curriculum:

> Majorities of superintendents and principals as well as about 40 percent of teachers in all three states reported that the academic rigor of the curriculum had changed for the better in the wake of state accountability. (Hamilton et al., 2007, pp. 54–5)

Teachers in Pennsylvania were less likely than in the other states to agree. Teachers were more likely to say that things changed for the better than for the worse in terms of rigor, focus on student learning, student focus on school work, students learning important skills and knowledge, principal's effectiveness as instructional leader, teachers' relationships with their students, and their own teaching practices. Other positives included coordination of math and science curriculum across grades and the extent of innovative instructional approaches. Taken with the rest of the findings of this study, these results seem incongruous.

There were mixed results in the RAND study on how teachers and administrators described the extent of benefit to students, from a low of 28 percent of California elementary school teachers to 77 percent of Georgia elementary principals (Hamilton et al., 2007). It is difficult to interpret these results, but perhaps not surprising that there would be such variation, since states have different standards, responded differently to the law, and have their own educational histories. Hamilton et al. found one trend of note in the data on educators' perceptions of accountability's effects:

> In general, the perception that academic rigor, teachers' focus on student learning, and actual student learning had changed for the better was more prevalent among superintendents than principals and was more prevalent among principals than it was among teachers. (p. 56)

Again, these results are difficult to interpret. Hamilton et al. found that most consistently, teacher morale had declined, but despite the lower morale,

> most principals and many teachers judged the overall effects of accountability to be positive. Principals were more positive than teachers

about the overall impact of the accountability systems, and Georgia
educators were more positive than educators in the other two states.
More than half of principals in all three states (73 percent in California,
59 percent in Georgia, and 65 percent in Pennsylvania) reported that
the state accountability system had been beneficial for students in their
school. In comparison, approximately one-third of teachers in California
and Pennsylvania and a little over half in Georgia agreed that, overall, the
state's accountability system has benefited their students. (p. 58)

While I would not characterize the data from teachers as being supportive of
accountability policy, it is very curious that despite low morale, even a slim
majority of teachers in one of the states would indicate that accountability
benefits students.

Improvement strategies

Accountability policy has had the effect of encouraging schools to use
particular strategies to inform their practice. McNeil (2000a, 2000b) early
on noted this phenomenon in states with accountability systems predating
NCLB, with increased resources devoted to test preparation materials and
pep rallies as the stakes of tests got higher, crowding out other instructional
objectives.

Hamilton et al. (2007) report a fairly common experience across the
sample of educators:

> more than 90 percent of principals in California, Georgia, and Pennsylvania
> reported using four common school improvement strategies, including
> matching curriculum and instruction with standards, using research
> to guide improvement efforts, providing additional instruction to low-
> performing students, and increasing the use of student achievement data
> to inform instruction. (pp. 61–2)

Used less frequently, but by majorities of educators, were district-required
progress tests.

The attention to tests and subject matter that appears on tests may
become what educators have referred to as "teaching to the test." Virtually
all principals reported that they helped "teachers identify content that is
likely to appear on the state test so they can cover it adequately in their
instruction" (Hamilton et al., 2007, p. 85), "discussed methods for preparing
students for the state test at staff meetings" (p. 85), and "distributed released
copies of the state test or test items" (p. 85), except in the case of copies of
state tests in California, where only a majority of principals released copies
of the state tests; many California principals told researchers that they didn't

distribute copies of the tests, because they thought it might lead to patterns in score responses and invite unwanted scrutiny.

The alignment of curriculum with standards and tested material has been a concern, with some states faulted for not moving quickly enough to align standards and testing, and some schools and districts faulted for not aligning their curricula to standards and testing (Hamilton et al., 2007). The RAND study found negative attitudes among educators when tests, standards, and curriculum are not all aligned; the researchers found some evidence that a district's math curriculum could be off by a whole year compared to the standards, leading to questionable test data and problematic performance by schools and district. Of the three states studied, it appeared that Georgia was experiencing the most alignment, with educators experiencing the most alignment, monitoring, and use of standards. A related phenomenon was observed as a downside of alignment: educators felt pressured to keep up with district pacing guides and interim assessment systems, and teachers felt they had to hurry and provide coverage of content without waiting for mastery. At the same time, there was widespread agreement that the pacing guides hold higher-level students back.

Constriction of curriculum

The phenomenon of constriction of the curriculum, early on referred to as curriculum "narrowing" (King & Mathers, 1997), was reflected in a survey of teachers in North Carolina. Curriculum narrowing was widespread under its accountability program in the mid-1990s; the survey revealed a widespread decline in the time devoted to the untested areas of science and social studies (Jones et al., 1999), and subsequent research confirmed the earlier findings (Jones et al., 2003).

School leaders' reasons for eliminating time for nontested subject matter took on many forms. Across the three states in the RAND study, educators reported instructional time changes that were all slanted toward tested areas (Hamilton et al., 2007), but the effects found in this study did not seem to be as stark as has been reported in individual cases.

Bubble-kid phenomenon

A phenomenon not widely reported in previous accountability systems became very popular after NCLB. After NCLB, it did not take schools very long to realize that percentage proficiency was not something that rose by applying equal attention to all students. Some students are more valuable in this process, the "bubble kids," with whom instructional effort could lead to the most rewards when rewards are based on increasing the percentage of proficiency. The percentage of principals who claimed that they "[e]ncouraged teachers to focus their efforts on students close to meeting the standards" (Hamilton et al., 2007, p. 85) were startling in the RAND study; in Georgia, 90 percent of elementary principals and 93 percent of middle-school principals indicated they did so; those percentages were not as high in California (85% of elementary principals, 94% of middle-school principals) or in Pennsylvania (77% of elementary principals, 57% of middle-school principals), but in nearly all cases, substantial majorities did so.

Hamilton et al. (2007) had this to say about this phenomenon:

> The focus on students near the proficient cut score also raises concerns about detrimental effects on low-performing students who are not seen as likely to achieve proficiency in one year. In the absence of incentives for raising their scores, there is a risk that resources will be diverted away from them as well. (p. 131)

The authors also imply that there are similar implications for high-performing students. Recall that the purpose of the RAND report is to recommend ways to make NCLB more accurately meet its policy objectives, which is why the interpretation is worded to reflect "absence of incentives"; presuming to still operate within the logic of rewards and sanctions, the interpretation presumes that additional incentives are needed to correct the problems with the incentives already in place.

Different types of schools

There is ample evidence that accountability policy affects public schools differentially. In their study of accountability policy in high schools, Carnoy et al. (2003) distinguish three types of schools by how their conditions and achievement relate to accountability policy: target schools, orthogonal schools, and well-positioned schools. Capacity, student population, and curriculum are factors that place the schools in their categories. And depending on their category, the authors argue, schools generally have different responses to the pressures of external accountability. The authors use the distinction between external accountability and internal accountability from Elmore's previous work (discussed earlier) to describe the difference between meeting the compliance demands of external accountability systems by raising test scores and developing internal accountability—the capacity to develop a consistent set of goals for students, curriculum and instruction that supports those goals, and an internal process of assessment that enables educators to monitor their progress in achieving those goals (Carnoy et al., 2003; see also Kozar, 2011). Since they studied states prior to NCLB, not all of the state accountability systems had high stakes attached to them.

Target schools

"Target schools" are the public schools whose low academic achievement is the target for standards-based school reform, and the many commentators in the media seem to have these schools in mind when they kvetch about American public education. These are for the most part (but not exclusively) urban schools that serve largely minority and low-income populations. Target schools are the schools that have been the most frequent candidates for experiments in reconstitution, managerial shuffling, and curriculum scripting. In Carnoy et al.'s (2003) study, target schools did especially well on external accountability measures under high-stakes conditions. Target schools, in other words, were the most willing to do what it took to raise test scores. However, the researchers found that it was much more difficult for schools to improve their internal accountability. They concluded that high-stakes accountability policy did not improve internal accountability in target schools in the states studied, and they note that the policy contained no corresponding effort to build capacity (Carnoy et al., 2003).

Orthogonal schools

"Orthogonal schools" are those whose missions or purpose do not align well with testing or state standards. These include some arts schools, alternative schools, or laboratory schools, but these features of their missions aren't as definitive as the extent to which the curriculum aligns with the state's curriculum and testing regimen. This is an important category for Carnoy et al. (2004), because one of their underlying arguments is that schools that work on their internal accountability are more likely to do well in external accountability schemes and at the same time build their capacity. The exception is with orthogonal schools, which due to the misalignment of curriculum with the testing regimen, could have high internal accountability but may nevertheless do poorly in an external accountability regimen.

Well-positioned schools

The "well-positioned schools" are those that Carnoy et al. (2003) describe as being positioned to do well in accountability schemes by virtue of their student populations and test score histories. These schools maintain their position to do well on standardized tests, because before the implementation of accountability policy, they already have the test scores that will enable them to comply with the state. Cozzolino and Bichsel (2010) describe a well-positioned school district in Pennsylvania as able to largely ignore its state's accountability policy, because its capacity and student population guarantees its compliance. Well-positioned schools further benefit when states lower minimum scores required for students to meet proficiency, because it enables a school that does nothing specifically to increase its test scores to raise its percentage of students who are proficient. As Cozzolino and Bichsel demonstrate, these conditions provide a well-positioned district the opportunity to position itself as having standards higher than the state minimum standards and to innovate around goals that may transcend the state standards.

Although they do not use the same categories as Carnoy et al. (2003), Hamilton et al. (2007) do make a distinction between schools and districts that succeed with achieving adequate yearly progress goals and those that do not. In one of the most interesting findings in their study, Hamilton et al. (2007) found that "administrators in districts and schools that made AYP held more positive views about the validity of state tests than administrators in districts and schools that did not make AYP" (p. 45). This held in all three states, but the differences in Pennsylvania were most stark: in districts that met AYP, 70 percent of Pennsylvania superintendents and 56 percent of principals agreed with the statement that "state assessment scores accurately reflect student achievement" (p. 148). In contrast, in districts that did not meet AYP, 6 percent of superintendents and 16 percent of principals agreed with that statement. Hamilton et al. explain why this is a problem: "for [standards-based accountability] to function most effectively, all stakeholders should endorse the measures of progress (the state assessments, in the case of NCLB). If they do not, it may undermine the functioning of the accountability system" (p. 45). An accountability system can become dysfunctional when educators have such drastic views of the accuracy of the system, making it more difficult to rally educators around collective responsibility across districts, an issue especially in Pennsylvania, which in many parts of the state has multiple school districts within the same communities that fall in starkly different categories in the accountability system. There is little motivation for a well-resourced district with high capacity to collaborate with a nearby low-performing district if the two districts disagree on the validity of the system that has placed the two districts in the distinct categories.

Cheating

High-profile cheating cases in Houston (Ravitch, 2010) and Atlanta (Wilson et al., 2011) and suspected cheating in the District of Columbia (Gillum & Bello, 2011) have brought attention to the desperate measures that some schools have taken to avoid high-stakes sanctions. As Ravitch points out, there are overt, illegal forms of cheating and more subtle forms of gaming the system. The more overt forms of cheating involve changing wrong answers after children have finished their tests or providing students with test questions ahead of time. More subtle cheating takes the form of giving students extra time to finish, encouraging them to check their answers, or leaving up materials on classroom walls that can help students. Ravitch is also concerned that state policies that exclude some children from testing or lowering proficiency scores borders on "institutionalized cheating" (p. 226). Overt cheating can be caught by testing companies who find inordinately large numbers of wrong-to-right answer erasures on tests, which seems to have been the method most at question in the Atlanta schools (Wilson et al., 2011) and what has raised questions in Washington, D.C. (Gillum & Bello, 2011).

The extent of cheating—whether subtle or overt—is unknown. A recent study in Arizona distinguished between various forms of cheating and sought to determine the prevalence of those forms (Amrein-Beardsley et al., 2010). To the overt forms of cheating (which they define as first-degree cheating) and more subtle forms (second-degree), they add as third-degree cheating many of the practices that Hamilton et al. (2007) found to be widespread in schools, such as teaching to the test and using test bank questions in practice teaching. In their own nonrepresentative sample of Arizona educators, Amrein-Beardsley et al. found the following:

> Respondents reported engaging in the following practices themselves, most to least: encouraging students to redo problems (16%), giving students extra time on the tests (14%), coaching students during tests (8%), and leaving materials on the walls during testing (8%). They reported least often changing student identification numbers in order to eliminate low-scoring students' results (0%). (p. 11)

The results were much higher when respondents were asked if they knew of others participating in cheating behaviors:

> respondents reported knowing of situations in which their colleagues encouraged students to redo test problems (39%), gave their classes extra time to complete tests (34%), wrote down questions to help prepare students for future tests (24%), wrote down vocabulary words for the same purposes (23%), and read questions aloud when not allowed to do so (23%). They reported least often knowing others who changed student identification numbers on test booklets to eliminate low scores (1%) and encouraged others to cheat (3%). Respondents who participated in this study knew of few colleagues (10%) who outright cheated, or cheated in the first degree. Respondents knew more of their colleagues who engaged in second (21%) and third degree (18%) cheating practices. (p. 11)

What happens to teachers?

While much of what I have discussed already has implications for teacher practices, there is more research that specifically addresses teachers. Taken together, this research calls into question the professional standing of teachers as a result of high-stakes accountability policy.

Teacher morale/teacher philosophy

The earliest studies to take on the effects of accountability policy addressed teacher morale. It was indeed the first measurable effect of accountability policy. As several studies have suggested, teachers are critical of the effects of high-stakes testing on their work. These studies document quantitatively and qualitatively the effects on teacher morale (Groves, 2002; Hoffman et al., 2001; Jones et al., 1999; King & Mathers, 1997; McNeil, 2000a, 2000b), with teachers finding it particularly difficult dealing with the stigma associated with school labels (Murillo & Flores, 2002).

The RAND study found faculty morale to be the most negative effect of accountability policy. That morale seems to be affecting teachers regardless of their school's AYP status suggests a profound and lasting effect on the teaching profession. "Interestingly, across all three states, teachers in schools that made AYP were just as likely if not more likely as teachers in schools that did not make AYP to report this negative impact on morale" (Hamilton et al., 2007, p. 57). The default philosophy of education that high-stakes accountability policy encourages is inconsistent with the educational philosophies of many teachers, many of whom would identify themselves as progressive teachers (Gunzenhauser, 2003). Hamilton et al. similarly present this interpretation for this view across differently positioned schools. Some of their data addresses this point directly:

> Only 30 percent of teachers in Pennsylvania and 29 percent of teachers in California agreed that the state accountability system supported their personal approach to teaching. Slightly more than one-half of the teachers in Georgia (52 percent) reported that the accountability system in that state supported their personal approach to teaching. Thus, many teachers were experiencing some conflict between their own approach and the approach that their state was asking them to adopt as part of the NCLB initiatives. For example, one California teacher told us, "I know that for teachers, it's this great big machinery that's hanging over your head. You know you've got to do this, you've got to do that, you've got to be this, you've got to be that, to the point where you sort of lose the focus of how about just exploring things for the kids." (Hamilton et al., 2007, pp. 57–8)

Ravitch (2010) argues that this is one of the more critical failures of high-stakes accountability policy, because it disables teachers from teaching the way that they know to teach.

That this issue is found across differently positioned schools is rather significant and transcends the surface emotional issue of "morale." Positioning morale as an issue of dissonance between the methods teachers are being asked to teach and the beliefs which teachers hold makes this concern a philosophical issue, which I address more thoroughly in a later chapter. Based on their study of teachers at two elementary schools, Mathison and Freeman (2003) offer the following interpretation:

> These teachers confront the dilemma of being a good teacher, a professional, and helping kids to succeed, which is marked by performance on state tests. What we saw repeatedly was that this dilemma is almost always solved in favor of the students, that teachers sacrifice their professional integrity in order to help every child be as successful as s/he can be on the tests, even when they lack faith in the indicator. (para. 11)

Teacher attitudes toward children

At first glance, it might not seem very important to attend to how teacher attitudes toward children have changed over time. However, as I show in the next two chapters, in ethics, the relationship between a teacher and student is the foundation for ethical relations. There is not much data on how accountability policy has affected student-teacher relationships, and that is a significant gap in the literature, because the guiding principle to "leave no child behind" (the original phrase from Marian Wright Edelman, the founder of the Children's Defense Fund) is itself an ethical commitment. How teachers orient themselves toward students also has implications for the kind of interventions they may attempt if students are not doing well. In contrast to what Mathison and Freeman (2003) found in their study, quoted just above, Hamilton et al. (2007) found the following:

> teachers reported that students' lack of basic skills, support from parents, and student absenteeism and tardiness hampered their efforts. One of the underlying principles of NCLB is that educators are expected to promote high levels of achievement despite these conditions, but our findings suggest that large numbers of educators have not adopted this view. (p. 132)

But it is not as simple as the policy having a negative effect on the relationships. Evidence suggests that it has complicated the relation in important ways. The dynamics are difficult to capture in survey questions, and as I mentioned, there has been little other research to guide us on this question.

Accountability as a philosophical problem

In this section I reframe the effects of high-stakes accountability policy as deeper, philosophical issues. Not much has been written about the particular philosophies of education of educators working in public schools. For many teachers, philosophy of education is a subject they studied while in their teacher preparation programs. Depending on where in the country or when they were prepared, they may have taken it as a stand-alone course or as folded into a more general course introducing them to the social foundations of education or to teaching as a profession. Many preservice teachers preparing portfolios for licensure or certification are required to write philosophies of education, and they often write them as statements about their beliefs about children. Rarely are students encouraged to incorporate substantive philosophical ideas about education into their statements.

A philosophy of education is more than a statement about beliefs about children. For many years, everyone's philosophy of education statement seemed to begin with the statement that "all children can learn," then reiterated that belief in several different ways and their faith that as a teacher of all children, learning would occur. Behind this pithy phrase that "all children can learn" is the commendable belief in the educability of all children, the value in teaching anyone who becomes one's student, and the determination that all children, regardless of race, ethnicity, ability, or social standing, are deserving of a strong and vital public education.

These are important values and taken together into "all children can learn" make a nice slogan. However, the slogan is not a philosophy of education, because it leaves "education" itself undefined and unspecified. A philosophy of education should instead define education and identify and explain its value. What is education for? What role does education play in one's life? What does it mean to learn? To teach? Where do and should we learn? A philosophy of education can address all forms of education in a person's life, not just what occurs in the confines of school. Whether we are talking about education that takes place in a movie theater, on the Internet, at home, or in a school, a philosophy of education should address the meaning and value of all of these experiences. Because in this book I am focusing on accountability policy for public schools, the philosophies of education that I refer to focus on education in schools; however, the reader should be mindful that a philosophy of education that is silent on the aspects of experience that occur outside of school is ignoring a large component of education.

To put it succinctly, a philosophy of education addresses *why* we educate so that we make better choices about *who, what, where, when,* and *how* we educate. A philosophy of education provides answers to significant questions about the purpose and value of education and the kinds of persons we wish to come out of education. As Neil Postman (1985) suggests:

> The question is not, Does or doesn't public schooling create a public? The question is, What kind of public does it create? A conglomerate of self-indulgent consumers? Angry, soulless, directionless masses? Indifferent,

confused citizens? Or a public imbued with confidence, a sense of purpose, a respect for learning, and tolerance? (p. 18)

Along with Elliot Eisner (2002), I assert that the lack of attention to these fundamental questions leads to aimless pursuits of school reform. In the rush to reform schools, too little emphasis is placed on the underlying philosophy of education that is being served. And also as Eisner advocates, the purpose and value of education should be the subject of community discussions:

We are not clear about what we are after. Aside from literacy and numeracy, what do we want to achieve? What are our aims? What is important? What kind of educational culture do we want our children to experience? In short, what kind of schools do we need? (p. 577)

As suggested by Postman (1995) and Eisner (2002), rich, dialogical responses to these questions should lead to richer and more purposeful educational experiences.

Because of the predominance of talk about accountability, standards, and student achievement, educators are willing (or are forced) to concede the definition of education and its value to whatever they are told it means. Implied in many policy statements about education is that it is essential to build a solid economy, as if the economy were more important than education. The push for a stronger economy is even more fervent considering the ongoing economic difficulties, unemployment and underemployment especially, following the recent recession. Economic purposes are certainly part of the value of the contribution that education makes, but if we begin to think about why we need a good economy, why people need jobs, why people need to support themselves, and why so many people seek careers, we might be able to redefine education and construe its value more broadly. One reason we pursue employment is for better quality of life, and for many of us, good work is a component of the quality of life. Or perhaps we pursue all of our tasks in life for the glory of God, in honor of our ancestors, or for the good of humanity. Whatever reasons we may articulate for our lives, once we engage in those conversations about why we do things, we can also consider the value that education provides in helping us reach those goals, for the joy it brings as a pursuit in and of itself, and how it participates in who we are and who we are becoming. Implied in this statement is something important: education can contribute not only to the intermediate things, like employment, which help us achieve quality of life, but education also makes a direct contribution to quality of life. Education is not just about the accumulation of knowledge, because knowledge is only one part of life. A philosophy of education should address the value of education for cultivating knowledge, morality, aesthetic experience, and whatever else we value as part of our being.

Once we begin to expand our notion of the meaning and value of education, we have the basis for a more robust and worthwhile philosophy of education. We can now return to the statement that "all children can learn" with a richer sense of why that slogan may be important as the mere beginning of a discussion about education. A more robust philosophy of education also gives us something more than naïve optimism to build upon. It arms us with stronger reasons for developing educational ideas—interesting methods of instruction, important concepts, invigorating experiences—that enable us to work toward the ultimate purposes that drive our work.

By this point, high-stakes accountability has so dominated discourse and practices in public education that dialogue about the purpose and value of education has been circumscribed to dangerously narrow proportions. As Siegel (2004) has argued, the manifestations of accountability systems, particularly in laws authorizing state accountability systems, fall far short of defensible educational ideals (see also Blacker, 2003). In his analysis of the use of the Florida accountability system, Siegel notes how the state derives its rationale for its accountability system and the use of the Florida Comprehensive Assessment Test solely from economic aims. The rationale is instrumental to economic ends, Siegel argues, and by failing "to recognize [students] as ends-in-themselves . . . treat[s] them immorally" (p. 60). Economic aims, while valuable themselves, are for Siegel morally inadequate as educational ideals. He explains what the economic rationale of the Florida accountability system lacks:

> it ignores widely acknowledged intrinsic . . . and more fundamental aims of education—for example, the enhancement of knowledge and understanding, the fostering of rationality and good judgment, the opening of minds and the overcoming of provincialism and close-mindedness, the enlargement of the imagination, the fostering of creativity, and so on. (p. 59)

Amid the litany of effects of accountability policy, it has become more difficult for substantive educational ideas to arise to the surface. The substance of the debate has been replaced with get-scores-quick schemes, like the series of miracles in states that have raised test scores, only to fall again, when it becomes clear that schools have in some way gamed the system, whether the illegal means coming to light in Atlanta or the other means, such as coaching kids to be better test takers or teaching narrow, tested content. Rarely are any ideas floated about the substantive value of reform efforts. Instead, educators and policy makers have been too willing to sacrifice their educational ideas on the altar of test scores.

As Hamilton et al. (2007) suggest, it is important to acknowledge how poorly that teaching practices made popular by high-stakes accountability compare to teachers' instructional beliefs. The encouraged default philosophy is antithetical to the progressive educational tradition (Vinson et al., 2004), arguably the most dominant (if misunderstood and misapplied) philosophy of education advocated by educators. John Dewey's (1966/1916, 1997/1938) educational philosophy cuts against the use of high-stakes accountability in at least three ways: the source of knowledge in experience, the necessity for fluidity of instruction, and the inherent significance of connection between the learner and content (Vinson et al., 2004). It is not my project to champion progressive education, for while a progressive education is what I prefer for myself and for my own children, there are multiple compelling philosophies of education that deserve adoption, experimentation, and propagation, including the conservative educational philosophies advocated by Diane Ravitch (2010) and E.D. Hirsch (1996). While it could be argued that a knowledge-based educational philosophy like Hirsch's could be seen as more amenable to a testing regimen, his content is tied to a particular psychology of the mind and psychology of learning that would not necessarily fit the grade-by-grade, standards-based approach that states mandate and test. Accountability policy, an educational policy that ostensibly advocates no particular educational philosophy, effectively obliterates all but an indefensible, default philosophy, limiting innovation to the well-positioned schools that need not worry about external accountability strictures.

For both progressives and conservatives, schools are public sites where communities come together in dialogue about fundamental questions associated with the purpose and value of education (Eisner, 2001, 2002; Postman, 1995; Ravitch, 2010; Rose, 2009), where the educational aims that Siegel (2004) mentions in the passage excerpted above are given appropriate hearing. In an ideal situation, philosophies of education are discussed, negotiated, put in process, tested, and revised. They involve a wide array of members of school communities, including educators, parents, students, and members of the larger community. For both progressives and conservatives, the underlying assumption of the significance of dialogue is emancipatory (or one might say freedom-constituting). Progressives and conservatives may articulate that emancipation differently, with conservatives identifying the essential features of the rational mind, tied to the enduring truths associated with Western culture. Progressives place greater emphasis on the underlying belief that education should enable persons to name their worlds and determine their destinies, individualized and contextualized in communities, and offering possibility as opposed to discipline (Greene, 1988; Freire, 2000/1970).

Two recent authors have crystallized their progressive (Noddings, 2007) and conservative (Ravitch, 2010) concerns with the philosophical implications of high-stakes accountability policy. Both are very critical of accountability policy, for many of the same reasons, although their solutions are distinct.

Progressive critiques of accountability policy

The progressive educational tradition takes its early form in the work of Dewey (1997/1938, 1966/1916), finds later (and different) form in Freire (2000/1970), Greene (1988), Postman (1995), Rose (1989, 2009) and Eisner (2001, 2002), among many others. The perspectives that Scott Fletcher (2000) identifies as "emancipatory" represent various possible philosophical groundings for multiple views that may be expressed in school communities. As a philosopher of education working in the progressive tradition, Nel Noddings (2007) is concerned with the ways in which NCLB (as an exemplar of the school reform movement that generated it) "misconstrues the aims of education and indeed misunderstands the very nature of education" (p. 7), because it attempts to apply the same standards to all students, regardless of their interests, abilities, and choices. This is a substantively philosophical difference that Noddings has with standards-based education, if standards end up being applied to everyone: "A system of schooling that provides few choices and fails to prepare its students to make well-informed choices in the future does not deserve the label *education*, and it undermines the liberal democracy it should support" (p. 7).

The rhetoric of accountability policy overtakes the philosophical justification for the kind of education it advocates, Noddings (2007) contends. She particularly takes issue with the "no excuses" sloganeering associated with attempts to defeat and discredit arguments that a standardized approach to education is fair and equitable. She argues against the suggestion that all students must master a common core of knowledge, particularly at higher levels, where it is patently false, for instance, that we should be pushing for all students to be ready for college.

Overemphasis on college preparation as the ideal aim of education forecloses other suitable possibilities. Noddings (2007) also argues against the economic-based arguments for higher levels of knowledge. "Too often, students are told that everyone now needs academic knowledge because we are living in a postindustrial, information age. But they are rarely given the actual figures on where the most jobs will be found" (p. 33). At the same time, Noddings is concerned about the other outcomes of education—"how to educate for citizenship, private life, moral life, spirituality" (p. 30)—educational concerns that largely fall outside the boundaries of testing regimens. Student interest, largely devalued, "by expending excessive time and energy coercing reluctant students to learn material they hate, we neglect those who love the material and could move through it rapidly and in far greater depth" (p. 31).

Progressive educators are interested in more holistic approaches to education. As Noddings (2007) suggests:

> We should want our children to develop as whole people—intellectually, morally, socially, emotional, artistically, spiritually. They should not

be treated as commodities for the labor and consumer markets. But unfortunately the overemphasis on grades and test scores may do exactly that. (p. 43)

Assessments of student performance are characteristically open-ended for progressive educators. For Noddings, there is an important distinction between two questions: the closed-ended question, "Has Johnny learned X?" and the open-ended question, "What has Johnny learned?" Progressive educators value the second question more than the first. The first is an important question, because there are many "concepts, definitions, and skills" that students should learn, but as she says, "these represent only the building blocks of lasting learning, and they will themselves be forgotten rapidly if not used regularly" (p. 44).

As a progressive educator, Noddings (2007) is suspicious of the maladaptive consideration of standards, which in most states are voluminous in content and inconsistent in their level of conception. Standard can mean a topic, concept, skill, or objective. And while the term "is meant to convey a twin sense of uniformity and high quality . . . the resulting masses of standards are really elaborate tables of contents and far too specific to be used with all students" (p. 52). Noddings describes the slow progression from behavioral objectives, through competencies, and then content standards. For her, it has been essentially the same idea, just subtly different language to fit the contemporary agenda. But it's not a trivial change, because the shift to the language of "standards" works toward the uniformity of outcome that as a progressive she argues against. A former math teacher, she nevertheless does not see the need for everyone to experience the same mathematics: "Labeling 'numbers and operations' and 'patterns, functions, and algebra' as standards instead of topics or subjects signals complicity with a movement that insists on filling those standards out with particular outcomes" (p. 54). After all students learn the basics, she prefers that educators be able to use their professional judgment on which courses and topics to offer that will fit the needs and interests of individual students. At the same time, she is just as skeptical of watered-down mathematics coursework that offers students nothing but a placeholder.

As an observer of the standards movement, Noddings (2007) critiques the misuse of testing and the overuse of the notion of grade level. What counts as "proficiency," she argues, is typically nothing more than the norm for the grade level. Without a reliable basis for determining what actually is appropriate for a student of a certain age and experience, "Most states have fallen back on norm-referenced thinking to establish a level of proficiency" (p. 65). Noddings has a clearer notion of proficiency:

The ideal would be to determine the score at which students might be assured of predictable success in future work or study, but we are a long way from having such information, and few policy makers are even asking the question. (p. 65)

Had schools a clear notion of proficiency, it might make sense for students to be held to that standard, but Noddings does not see the value in putting children who fail to make a cutoff score into an intensive "drill and kill" environment, without individualized instruction, to get them to pass the test the next time.

To conclude Noddings' progressive position, she argues also that the goals of any reform movement need to be based on moral ends. The high-standards movement ostensibly starts off with the high moral ground—a dual concern for quality and equity, which had been positioned as opposing concerns. The failing of NCLB was the lack of attention to the moral grounding of the means to which its ends would be reached:

> It is not just educational ends that must be morally justified; our means must also pass a moral test. If the means chosen cause sleeplessness and nausea, increased boredom, poorer relationships, reduced thinking, and lower creativity, they must be rejected. . . . In the process, we should avoid dehumanizing teachers and students and explore new ways to educate for genuine intellectual growth, moral commitment, and democratic citizenship. (Noddings, 2007, pp. 80, 83)

Conservative critiques of accountability policy

An alternative to progressivism is conservatism, or what Fletcher (2000) calls neoconservatism. He names Chester Finn and William Bennett as influential figures; others are Allan Bloom, Hirsch, and Ravitch. Fletcher summarizes that "a key proposition defended by neoconservatives is that disciplinary knowledge, which rests in teachers and texts, should be the fundamental organizing principle of curriculum" (p. 13). Neoconservatives are most likely to support the place of high-stakes testing in programs for accountability, and at the same time, they are the strongest supporters of the neoclassical philosophy of education. These two beliefs have come into conflict for some conservatives, including Ravitch. The neoclassical approach is to defend the rigor and value of academic disciplines, but an effect of high-stakes accountability policy is to place greater emphasis on the measurement of achievement than the knowledge itself.

I should note that the terms progressive and conservative as I use them here do not map on to the liberal/conservative dualism that is the mainstay of popular political discourse. NCLB was in fact an example of bipartisan legislation that drew in both liberal and conservative policy makers, notably Senator Edward Kennedy. Beliefs about educational philosophy do not follow the same liberal/conservative divide. Ravitch throughout her career has been critical of progressive education, and she is at times as dismissive of high-stakes accountability policy as she continually has been about progressive education. Ravitch's (2010) criticism of NCLB points out an important difference between at least two groups of political conservatives who initially supported NCLB: those for whom the implementation of high standards was the most important feature (e.g., Ravitch, 2010), and those for whom the stipulation for privatization solutions to the cost and quality of education was the most important feature (e.g., the Heritage Foundation). The latter are referred to as either neoconservative or neoliberal, depending on the context and which aspect of the "choice" agenda is emphasized.

In perhaps the most comprehensive genealogy of standards, testing, and choice reform yet written, educational historian (and former assistant secretary of the U.S. Department of Education), Ravitch (2010) summarizes the roots and turning points of the related movements for test-based accountability, standards-based reform, and the proliferation of initiatives to promote school choice. She thoroughly traces the exercises of power behind the scenes that led to NCLB as opposed to other educational reforms. Most troubling for her are the antidemocratic outcomes of these movements, notably the outsized policy influence increasingly enacted by private foundations (the new breed of "venture philanthropists" like Eli Broad, Bill Gates, and the Walton Family), the dumbing-down of educational standards, and the systematic decimation of public school systems, particularly in urban communities (see also Meier & Wood, 2004; Ricci, 2004). She points to the disproportionate concentration of students with special needs (she notes students who are English-language learners and students who qualify for special education services) as being largely pushed out of charter schools, the reform method favored by powerful foundations. She predicts this outcome for NCLB: "Charter schools in urban centers will enroll the motivated children of the poor, while the regular public schools will become schools of last resort for those who never applied or were rejected" (p. 220).

Ravitch's persistent cause throughout her career has been curriculum quality and the selection of materials in English literature and social studies education that transmit cultural heritage and promote civic engagement. She argues that competition and choice, the business and management-minded educational reforms, are antithetical to public responsibility for education.

Management-based approaches are also subject to Ravitch's critique. She recalls the progression of model educational reforms from New York City's District 2 to San Diego Unified School District, then the mayor-led New York City and Washington, D.C. reform strategies. As Ravitch describes them, each of these efforts follows a pattern of autocratic control by a chief executive, demands for test score results, initial rises in scores, high-profile leadership departures, and subsequent test score declines. Ravitch faults arrogance of leadership and nondemocratic governing practices. She is especially critical of school leaders who are not accountable or transparent to democratically elected boards. A pillar of conservative educational reform has been strong leadership, and so her criticisms, while they stay true to her push for excellence and high standards, cleaves her from neoliberal reformers focused on market-based solutions.

As a former proponent of the choice strategy, Ravitch's critiques highlight the inconsistencies of the accountability policy. Ravitch calls for greater accountability for the public dollars being spent on market-derived reforms that prove to be no more effective than what we had before. This kind of additional accountability (political accountability at the highest levels) is partly what Ravitch calls for and why she insists that there be more respect for the public in public schools, mayoral control in New York and Michelle Rhee's tenure as chancellor of the District of Columbia Public Schools being Ravitch's prime counter examples. Although one can see a potentially new route in the accountability discourse, with the public awakened to such curiosities as the tremendous wealth generated privately by accountability policy, Ravitch has generated few allies among conservative educational reformers.

Ravitch's current lack of conservative allies may be due to a neoliberal dominance of the conservative movement, or perhaps because few policy makers have been forthcoming with alternatives. As remedies for NCLB, Ravitch's (2010) ideas fall into two general categories. The first is the smarter use of standardization, effectively fixing the loopholes in laws that allow states to dumb down their standards, write easy tests, and manufacture indefensible scores for what counts as proficiency. Ravitch advocates what we might call the Massachusetts approach, reflecting the praise she gives that state for high standards, aligned testing, and rigorous accountability. The second is a conservative call for rich and classic content, a fundamentally knowledge-based approach to education which Ravitch has been consistently arguing for in contrast to method-driven approaches to learning that at times de-emphasize the importance of knowledge of particular facts.

Ravitch's critique is a story of conversion, of coming to realize that the ideas which she had espoused were not working out in practice. Much of Ravitch's criticisms of NCLB and *Race to the Top* were presaged prior to the implementation of the former, with even early advocates of the high-standards movement arguing that the demands of external accountability schemes that several states had implemented prior to NCLB were not systematically leading to increased capacity, but were instead causing educators to work harder at what they were already doing (Elmore & Fuhrman, 2001) and granting outsized influence to test score performance. Reforms designed to force schools to raise test scores were evaluated by policy makers largely on their ability to force scores to rise, and even the lack of concurrent rises on different tests, such as the National Assessment of Educational Progress, did not keep high-stakes accountability programs from being adapted nationally (Sirtonik, 2002, 2004).

In contrast to Ravitch, other conservatives generally follow the neoliberal agenda of privatization as the method of choice for educational reform. Chester Finn (2010) is a conservative ally of Ravitch in educational excellence initiatives going back to the 1980's. In his review of Ravitch's book, he rebrands himself a radical and Ravitch a conservative. His contrast to Ravitch is twofold and it reflects the direction that educational policy reform seems to be going. First, he interprets the effects on schools and teachers as indications of the inherent corruption in the educational system:

> failures of recent years have left me angrier than ever with that system, its adults-first priorities, its obduracy, inertia and greed, as well as its capacity to throw sand into the gears of every effort to set it right. Unlike Diane, I don't trust teacher unions to do right by children (or to do right by great teachers, for that matter); I don't expect locally elected school boards to put kids' interests first; I see "neighborhood schools" as education death traps for America's neediest youngsters; and I think the "Broader, Bolder" social-reform agenda is on the one hand naive (most of these things just aren't going to happen on their own and can't be made to happen) and on the other deeply mischievous (because it lifts responsibility from schools for all that they could and sometimes do accomplish pretty much single handedly). (para. 10)

Finn (2010) characterizes Ravitch as wishing for a "restoration," which is in some aspects correct, because Ravitch has at least three restorations in mind: a restoration of knowledge-based education with high standards, a restoration of democratic accountability for school decision-making, and a restoration of respect for the teaching profession. Finn summarizes his stated agenda as "more fundamental and radical reform," including expanding school choice, "stronger (and broader) external standards," "more open paths to becoming an educator," "empowered school leaders (*really* empowered, in ways that would also break the union stronghold) who are compensated like CEOs," "super pay for greater instructors and no pay for incompetents," "a complete makeover of 'local control,'" and "a shakeup from top to bottom" (para. 11).

Upon closer inspection, the disagreement between Ravitch and Finn that is embedded in the summary of his agenda is limited to the forms of leadership desired for school districts, the expansion of choice in the form of charter schools, and the push to break the union stronghold. Ravitch has marshaled evidence that these three specific initiatives have centrally failed in their promise to bring about intended reform. In his brief review, Finn does not engage her evidence or challenge her interpretations of her evidence. It has, in fact, few characteristics of a book review. Finn provides instead a glimpse at the conservative agenda for school reform moving forward, and it is an embrace rather than a critique of the principles of NCLB, with an implied interpretation that schools are to blame for the consequences of the policy.

Philosophy of education as reform moves forward

Philosophers of education seem to make pessimistic educational policy prognosticators, perhaps because they tend to focus on the extent to which educational practice falls short of its educational ideals. As educational policy moves forward, it does seem that educators can expect more of the same conditions that have been associated with the high-stakes accountability movement. Despite evidence of the negative effects of high-stakes testing coupled with standards-based reform in the states that had already adopted the twin reforms, NCLB became law, and high-stakes accountability policy became law in all 50 states. And despite evidence that the policy was built upon inaccurate assumptions about what motivates educators to improve their practice, the policy is likely to persist.

Despite Ravitch's confident and persistent voice (she continues to appear on television and has written opinion pieces prolifically ever since, and her book came out in paperback in Fall 2011, 18 months after its hardback publication) and her continual criticism of the educational agenda of President Barack Obama, she draws few allies in powerful policy circles. Evident in the *Race to the Top* educational reform policy are the three pieces of Finn's agenda that make him distinct from Ravitch. Julie Underwood's (2011) analysis of the manner in which state education policy agendas are being informed by the American Legislative Exchange Council (ALEC) suggests that Finn's agenda is right in line with the direction educational policy is going to go. There appears to be no opposition in national leadership, perhaps because accountability has played out as a failure, and proponents of the ideas are either bailing out or digging in their heels.

All of the discussion in this chapter suggests that high-stakes accountability policy raises serious questions for advocates for both progressive and conservative philosophies of education, and the numerous effects of accountability policy raise a number of ethical issues that we as educators will have to address. Based on what has emerged for future educational policies, it seems that the need to address the dangers associated with high-stakes accountability will continue. Based on the emerging research about high-stakes testing, it has become very difficult for educators to enact philosophies of education. The narrowing of the conversation about the purpose and value of education requires attention at the national and state level to lower the stakes of testing, because it puts in place a default philosophy of education that is indefensible. At the school level, it is essential that schools maintain dialogue among the various members of the school community about the purpose and value of schooling and not allow themselves to settle for the default philosophy of education.

The push for accountability has privileged knowledge and skills that are measurable on tests, which we have known to be a danger of high-stakes accountability policy since before NCLB. More so, in the response to NCLB, schools (especially target schools but not exclusively) have systematically rearranged themselves for better knowledge acquisition, without attention to the human toll: without sufficient public deliberation about their implied aims for children, without attention to how educators and school leaders are being cultivated as moral actors, and without attending to what might be done differently.

3
Ethics in educational practice

Irreverent Sid

Sid Davidson is an elementary principal we interviewed during his first year of working in a new district. Like many principals in Western Pennsylvania, Sid is young, energetic, and smart. He has the additional gift of irreverence. His interview is filled with expletives, confessions, and quick stories of compelling ethical dilemmas. Sid works in a district where the schools do not always meet the demands of external accountability. The median income in his district is about average for the county in which it is located. There is a mix of races and income levels in his school, and the year prior to the interview, his school did not meet its test score targets for all his subgroups, including children who have an IEP. He explains it this way:

> My school is going to be on the warning list because of our subgroups. As a whole our school did score well above AYP, but our subgroups didn't make it. Our African American kids didn't make it. Our IEP kids didn't make it. Our free and reduced lunch kids didn't make it. For some reason, those are like the same kids. Our African American boys. . . . They are also the same ones with IEPs and free and reduced lunch.

As he continues his story, Sid explains the temptation to blame the students for their test scores. One of Sid's concerns is that his school and his teachers may appear racist, since he and most of his teachers are white, and the students who are not making progress are African American. He sees no evidence of explicit racism among his teachers, as he explains, and then he describes how the scores of a small number of children affect his school's status on the Pennsylvania System of School Assessment (PSSA):

> I've never heard a single derogatory comment about those kids [from the teachers]. . . . Those kids make gains and we do—for all of our learning support kids—we do progress monitoring to show on a graph where they're at in reading, and this is how much they've increased. And all of our kids are making progress and we can show that, but it doesn't matter on PSSA. And if you break down the number, it's really close. It comes down to something like six kids. There are six kids in my building who caused our scores in those subgroups to be below the benchmark. So then next year, if those six kids don't improve or we get a couple other kids, my school is going to be placed on "School Improvement." What do you want me to do about that?

At this point Sid comes up with a hypothetical answer to his rhetorical question, since he is aware what the threat of being placed in the "School Improvement" category could encourage a principal to do:

> And that's when you get [the idea that] maybe I should call those parents and tell them to keep the kids home that week. It would fix my problem. Maybe that kid needs to get chicken pox that week, you know. Maybe I just need to have those six kids sit in the office and watch cartoons that week. Because I have a 99 percent participation rate, I can afford to lose six kids in my participation rate. We could play those games—we don't—but if I thought I was going to lose my job over it, I might.

Sid's teachers and his own children hate that the tests take a week away from learning. His irreverence gets him in trouble, like when the district curriculum coordinator "yelled" at him for equating the PSSAs with the film, *The Matrix:*

> When I entered the central [district] building I [talked] to the curriculum director about how I was entering the matrix—a place where I had to pretend to care about standardized tests. And I had to go over there and say how much I loved them and how I had this plan for improving them.

Another interaction with the curriculum director left him incredulous. An avid reader with a well-developed bullshit detector, Sid questions the evidence that supports the district's reading program, and he is suspicious of a new testing system the state was piloting at the time, the Pennsylvania Valued-Added Assessment System (PVAAS). Sid did some background checking on the PVAAS and found that it was based on a system developed in Tennessee to determine which teachers were substandard. He described the encounter with his friend, the curriculum director:

> I tried to get the curriculum director to explain this to me, and that is when he told me that if my attitude about PSSA tests didn't change, my tenure at [my current district] would be a very short one. . . . I just laughed and said "are you threatening me?" Because there is no way that he can rid of me. . . . And he said, "No, I'm just trying to give you some advice because the superintendent's job is directly related to how well we score on PSSAs, and if you're not scoring well, she's going to make your life hell. So you better get on board with this." Because I was saying things like "It's government surveillance. I can't believe you don't see this." The other thing that they told me was that the principalship was not a platform to be able to dispute these things or fight these things. You just go along with what you're told.

Sid is more experienced (and more subversive) to take his friend's advice. His educational history suggests that he knows the kind of educator he wants to be. Sid said this about his philosophy of education:

> I became a teacher because I had a lot of crummy teachers. . . . Nobody should have to have teachers like the ones that I had. So part of my philosophy would have to be: I want the kids to feel comfortable. I want them to feel safe. I want the kids to get excited about learning.

Following the advice of one of his university professors, Sid sees his job as principal as facilitating teachers' work, "to help remove the hurdles that teachers face every day in order to do their jobs. So I tell them that at the beginning at every year, 'That's what I'm here for. I'm here to help you.'"

This philosophy comes up in interesting ways. One of his teachers came to him about a scripted mathematics program that had students chanting 50 math facts over and over again. When he overheard it as he walked down the hall, Sid thought it sounded like a prophet leading a cult.

> And I said to the teacher, "What they hell are you doing"? And she said, "This is what we're supposed to do. It's the curriculum. But I don't like it." And I said, "Am I collecting this? Are you grading this or turning this in to anyone?" And she said, "No." . . . . And I said, "Well, why don't you close your door, and I don't need to know that. So if you don't think it's good, then don't do it." But they don't [close their doors] anymore. They are afraid. Teachers don't feel comfortable doing that anymore. The new PVAAS thing is going to add to it and the surveillance we do to them through PSSA.

The role of ethics in schools under the pressure of accountability

In this story, Sid provides multiple examples of instances when he, his teachers, and his curriculum director respond to the pressures of external accountability with varied ethical implications. Sid provides his teacher a moral justification for not complying with the district's mathematics curriculum. He suggests that if the teacher believes the chanting is not a good method, then she is justified in not complying, and on top of that, he gives her a strategy for hiding it from him. At the same time, he is acting under a set of limitations himself. Warned unofficially by his friend, the curriculum director, Sid is in a tight position; and he is told (he does not indicate by whom) that as principal he is not in a position to resist; actually, the message is that he is not in a position to lead. He also identifies a moral stand he takes by identifying a dishonest strategy for gaming the system (arranging for a small group of students to not take the tests) and arguing against it. And although I am confident based on my knowledge of Sid that his remark about chicken pox is a conjecture intended to highlight the absurdity of his situation, it is nevertheless a chilling thought. Perhaps most significant in the story is that Sid admits that he could imagine conditions (where high stakes would amount to him losing his job) under which he might be more tempted to do something to remove the six children from his testing group.

Sid's stories are more colorful than most that I have heard over my time interacting with educators about accountability policy, but his experiences are fairly common, particularly among educators who work in districts where schools may at times or on some measures not meet the demands of external accountability systems. His story demonstrates numerous ethical dilemmas that educators face on a daily basis, and how surveillance and high stakes complicate those dilemmas. In this chapter, I provide some background on ethical theory to explain the extent to which ethics as we have traditionally understood it in education has helped—but not completely—how educators respond to the challenges of being a professional educator. But first, I very briefly summarize the various ways that educational theorists have approached these issues in the most recent literature on ethical teaching and ethical leadership.

Ethical frameworks in education

Educators who write about professional ethics rarely fit neatly into one of the meta-ethical traditions that I describe in the next section of this chapter. As Felicity Haynes (1998) argues, "in a complex world, competing coherent systems will require ongoing negotiation for the competing merits of different conceptions of ethics" (p. 19). When we explore moral issues in education, the strengths and weaknesses of each of the traditions suggest that a multifaceted approach to ethics is most appropriate. Most of those who write about ethics in educational practice argue that it should be fundamental to educational practice, and I fall in with that considerable company.

I have included in the reference list of this book work that centers the importance of ethics for educational practice, and all are especially recommended as resources for making ethics central to educational practice:

- Gary Anderson (2009) addresses the dangers of high-stakes accountability policy and explains his vision for "advocacy leadership" grounded in Freire's (2000/1970) philosophy of education;
- Roland S. Barth (2001) focuses on relationships and also advocates that we "think otherwise" about our educational practices, particularly in light of demands that seem to conflict with our beliefs;
- Lynn Beck (1994) applies Noddings' (1984) ethic of caring to school administration;
- Gert Biesta (2006) argues that we should go "beyond learning" in how we think about educational practice;
- Paulo Freire (2000/1970) centers the pedagogical relation in his philosophy of problem-posing education (the pedagogy of the oppressed) and has influenced a broad scholarship building upon the integrity of the pedagogical relation;
- Michael Fullan (2003) argues for the moral imperative of school leadership;
- Felicity Haynes (1998) draws from a broad range of ethical theory, including post-structural ethics, to argue for an ethics of consequences, consistency, and care;
- Craig Johnson (2012) uses Parker Palmer's metaphor of casting light (as opposed to casting shadow) to frame his comprehensive analysis of leadership;
- Robert Nash (2002) explains how "three moral languages"—rules and principles, character, and basic beliefs—can be brought to bear on ethical issues and professional practices;
- Nel Noddings (1984) articulates her ethic of care (explained below) and in other work builds a philosophy of education based on that ethic (Noddings, 1992);
- David Purpel (1989) reclaims the value of spirituality for educational practice with a vision for resolving what he sees as a moral crisis in education;

- Thomas Sergiovanni (1992) influenced a generation of educational leadership scholars with his articulation of moral leadership for centering the practice of school administration;
- Robert Starratt (2004) centers the moral purposes of schooling (building on Sergiovanni [1992]), articulating a theory of ethical leadership based on virtues of responsibility, authenticity, and presence;
- Barbara Stengel and Alan Tom (2006) provide a comprehensive analysis of moral education and its various possible relations to academic education;
- Ken Strike (2006) bases his ethics for school leadership partly on John Rawls' social ethics.

Three plus two ethical traditions

The discipline of ethics within philosophy asks fundamental questions about the "good." Meta-ethics is the branch of that discipline that seeks to define the basic question "What is good?" and its variants, such as: What does it mean to lead a good life? What are the characteristics of a good person? How do we determine when our actions are good? What are the grounds upon which one may defend one's actions as good? In general, ethicists are interested in moral goods—those actions, qualities, or outcomes that we believe we ought to do, have, or effect (things that we may say have moral value)—as opposed to nonmoral goods, which are things that we may say have value, but not moral value. Robert Nash, one of my former professors, makes the distinction with the examples of the moral value of courage and the nonmoral value of chocolate.

Philosophers of education address these and other questions about ethics in relation to education: What place does ethics have in a philosophy of education? To what extent is ethics important for teaching practice? When in an educator's professional life does ethics make a difference? What does an educator need to know about ethics to be an effective educator? These are all questions that come up in my graduate course in professional ethics. Educators who take an ethics course as an elective seem generally predisposed to the idea that ethics is important. But quite often, students find ethics to have a rather limited role in their practice. In some cases, educators believe that ethics is synonymous with the law, and they look to the law for guidance on how they should act. Still others see ethics as an imposition, particularly when I ask students to define the related terms "ethics" and "morals."

When students define "ethics," they connect the term to specific expectations that society has for professionals in professional settings, such as codes of ethics. When students define "morals," the term (or its variant, morality) is usually reserved for prescriptive standards of behavior imposed by some powerful entity. For these students, they consider the latter term to be outdated and dogmatic. The etymology of both terms is tied to codes of behavior, with "ethics" coming from Greek and "morals" coming from Latin. Philosophers sometimes make a distinction between the two terms, often to distinguish between professional or public behavior (for ethics) and private behavior (for morals), but those distinctions are not consistent in the philosophical literature. Instead, common use has made preference for one term or the other contextual. We usually refer to statements about the expected behavior of professionals as "codes of ethics," but these codes typically are confined to specific professional contexts, and some personal "moral issues" are not considered relevant. In the context of this sentence, ethics and morals can be said to overlap, but the distinction made in the sentence is not consistent in all other uses of the terms. I do not resolve the distinction for this book, and I do not believe that it is necessary. In this book, I use the terms in the overlapping senses that philosophers typically do, and I do not expect the reader will find much meaning in any distinctions I make between their uses.

There are three main ethical traditions in Western philosophy. William Frankena (1973) describes them as deontological ethics, consequentialist ethics, and virtue ethics. To those three categories, especially for their applications to education, I would add relational ethics and post-structural ethics. These are meta-ethics, or theories about ethics. After reading about them more in depth, students generally find themselves at home in one of the ethical traditions more than others. For each ethical tradition, I summarize its strengths and weaknesses, then describe the value that educators can draw from that ethical tradition. I also then use the language of the ethical tradition in relation to Sid's story, showing how Sid and his colleagues might use the theory, or how we might use the theory to interpret the situations he describes.

Deontological ethics

Moral principles are the basis of deontological ethics, and rules and duties are the basis for moral actions. Deontological ethicists consider these principles to be universal and categorical, and in ethical conflicts, deontological ethicists argue over which rule or principle should be more prominent. This tradition places primary importance on clear, rational thinking, and the notion of free will: one chooses to do what is right through principled reasoning. The primary example is Immanuel Kant (1996/1797), who argued for universalism (the idea that a moral principle is applicable to everyone) and the categorical imperative (the idea that a moral principle is applicable in every situation). Typical criticisms of deontological ethicists are that there is not much guidance when moral principles come into conflict, and the abstract nature of the principles suggests that the context of an ethical situation does not matter. The requirement of rationality also makes it seem like ethical action is a solely intellectual exercise.

From deontological ethics, an educator can draw on the importance of ethical ideals, the abstract and enduring concepts that we learn from tradition. Many educators who consider themselves religious identify with this tradition, particularly if they also consider themselves fundamentalists. For them, the deontological tradition can provide them a way of using their foundational beliefs to build their ethics (and there are numerous religious ethicists in the deontological tradition). At the same time, critiques of this tradition can enable an educator with strong principles to see how his practice may come in conflict with others who do not hold the same basic beliefs, a situation we should expect to find in a pluralist society in which others do not always share our beliefs. An educator may also find it impossible to act ethically as a deontological ethicist if the conditions under which the educator operates are irrational or contradict the educator's moral principles.

In Sid's story, we can see that Sid's principles are challenged by the system in which he is operating. Multiple duties are implied in his story: his duty to the six children who have a right to an education, his duty to the state to be honest, his duty to protect his teachers and his students from harm, and his duty to provide a complete and challenging education to all children. We might also say he has a duty to speak his mind as a professional with a master's degree and principal certification, a duty that we would want to be universal; we would want someone in a position of leadership to lead in a professional manner. The story does not mention Sid's family, but we would also say that he has a duty to provide for his family. These duties come into conflict at just about every turn. How can Sid balance all of these duties? To what degree would we expect Sid to act to change what is happening in his school? Do we know enough about his situation to know what would happen if Sid were to take a stand that his superiors disagreed with? How comforting would a principled stand be for Sid if it led to his being fired and being replaced by a more compliant principal? Is it a coincidence that principal and principle are words that are often confused?

It would appear that a principle-based ethics is difficult to enact in a context where compromises of principle have already occurred. We might assume from this story that a principle-based ethics is not possible in a school district whose practices are designed to ensure that the school and the district comply with the state's accountability system. Or, we might be led to believe that a principle-based ethics is a privilege available only to educators in well-positioned school districts that do not have the same worries as Sid. Also, this tradition might give us a reason to understand why Finn (2010) is so willing to blame schools for their failing to improve under high-stakes accountability policy.

Consequentialist ethics

Another modernist tradition is a direct critique of deontological ethics, particularly the importance of the particular situations of ethical dilemmas and the outcomes of our actions. Consequentialists offer the insight that following principles leads to unequal distribution of nonmoral goods, like happiness and wealth. Consequentialist (or teleological or utilitarian) ethicists argue that the outcomes of our actions should be the basis for determining the good. The view is often summarized in the phrase "the greatest good for the greatest number" (the basis of the principle of utility) and arises from a concern with egalitarianism. Examples are found in John Stuart Mill (1993/1871) and Peter Singer (see Taylor, 2009). Standard criticisms arise from the observation that acting ethically seems to require knowledge of all possible outcomes, which some deem impossible and others deem impossibly constrained by cultural expectations. Particularly in the form of utilitarianism, consequentialist ethics seems to make the moral good to be secondary to the equal distribution of nonmoral goods. Or, it may seem to displace the notion of the good to a social theory about egalitarianism. Also, utilitarianism in particular seems to be overly focused on ethical dilemmas, without providing much guidance on day-to-day life, where the principle of utility might not seem to be at issue very often.

From the consequentialist ethics, the educator can draw the importance of the consequences of one's actions and the justification for a public education that serves all children to the best of their abilities. A moral actor can make the notion of consequences as complicated as she would like, considering even what kind of society she helps to create by acting the way she does in a certain situation. In that sense it can form the basis for a social ethics. At the same time, the critiques of utilitarianism in particular make it clear that the consequences of one's actions are not always clear; it requires quite a bit of knowledge about a situation and assumptions about how other people are going to act. Prejudicial thinking can lead a diehard consequentialist to make self-righteous decisions, and we can imagine that in education, we might never even know the ultimate consequences of those actions, particularly if we are in the position in making decisions based on what we believe will lead to the best outcomes for children in the future.

Returning to Sid's story, it now seems to be quite a bit about consequentialist ethics. Nearly everyone in his story is concerned about the consequences of their actions. Nearly everyone is inhibited in his or her actions because of anticipation of the consequences. We might imagine that key actors in the story have calculated the consequences of their actions and chosen to acquiesce (the teachers who chant the curriculum they do not believe in). We could ask each of them their reasoning. Perhaps they have reasoned that they suspect that their students will receive some sort of dire consequence if they don't do better on the PSSAs. Or, maybe they would make themselves too nervous to not do the chanting and cannot stand the pressure. In all of these possibilities, it is not clear which consequences are real ones and which are not, and it is not clear that teachers are really in a position to confidently resist in the way that Sid suggests they do. Also, is Sid really in danger of being fired for his irreverence? (In 2011, he was still employed there). In this story, the indeterminacy of consequences seems to be a compelling problem for making use of consequentialist ethics. If the situation were more predictable, we might find it more applicable.

Virtue ethics

Typically starting from the observation of Aristotle that characteristics of moral persons develop through cultivating virtues that are each the golden mean between two vices, virtue ethicists focus upon moral character as the basis for ethics. Examples are found in Aristotle (throughout his work, but *Nicomachean Ethics* [1962] is most often cited and read) and Alasdair MacIntyre (1981). The classic example of virtue is courage, which is not explicitly definable ("courage is the quality that we assign to people who are courageous" is about the closest we can come), but can be described as a golden mean between cowardice (its more direct opposite) and foolhardiness (a cumbersome word we make up because we do not often think of someone as being "too courageous"). Aristotle tells us that it is significant when one vice occurs to us more easily than the other; the more obvious vice is the one we should more assiduously avoid.

Critics of virtue ethics argue that the golden mean is difficult to find, is tautological, or could easily fall back upon what a society deems appropriate or desirable, suggesting that the good changes over time and in different cultures. Philosophers tend not to like cultural relativism with their traditional ethical theory, so that is a difficult criticism to swallow. Some ethicists are troubled by how much the virtue ethicist focuses on the ethical actor and not those who may be benefitted or harmed by the ethical actor. Further, we could imagine a society out of convenience making a virtue (being a benevolent slave holder, for instance) out of something that proves subsequently to be a vice, and it would be rather difficult to argue against it until people already disapproved of it, providing us with a chicken and egg problem: do people disapprove of slavery because it is wrong, or is slavery wrong because people disapprove of it? Virtue ethicists are not as interested in those kinds of trick questions but instead focus on the ineffable nature of the good and the insight that ethics is something that we constantly work at.

From the tradition of virtue ethics, educators may acknowledge the importance of the cultivation of one's moral characteristics through the decisions, both big and small, that one makes in one's life. Deciding the right path may mean modeling one's behavior after an admired mentor and cultivating in oneself the characteristics that that mentor has. The virtuous educator can see compromises he makes that detract from his character as faults that need to be corrected the next time a situation arises. In virtue ethics, there is not much need to distinguish between one's personal and professional life. Virtues can be seen to transfer from one situation to the next. From the critiques of the virtue ethics tradition, educators might be watchful that they not focus so much on themselves but on how their actions are benefitting or harming others. Although a virtue ethicist might find a great deal of comfort in the character education literature, the virtues that he possesses might end up clouding his judgment about which virtues his students would like to pursue or whose parents might like them to pursue. It can be difficult to separate the development of virtues with the concept of control, or with privilege (see Noblit and Dempsey [1996], for a stunning critique of the virtues inculcated in two segregated public elementary schools in adjoining neighborhoods that were combined into one integrated school).

At Sid's school, the language and concepts of virtue ethics might cause us to be concerned right away about the courage of the various actors, since courage is the classic example of virtue. Courage is not the only virtue and could be easily overplayed in this situation. The adults in the story seem to be stressed by the situation in which they have found themselves. We would probably get a lot of interesting additional stories out of the teachers in this school if we asked them what kind of persons they believed they were becoming by working in a school that asked them to teach in ways that they did not like. It would be vital to know what continual decisions they make with the curriculum and how they make it, perhaps even focusing on how well they feel who they are personally is reflected in their professional lives. We might be able to pinpoint how the conditions in which they are teaching are affecting them as virtuous persons. However, arguably the most important set of virtues in the school are the ones that are being cultivated in the students. What virtues are the adults modeling for the students and encouraging through the curriculum? To what extent are the difficulties the teachers having with the curriculum affecting the students? What is it they are learning? Virtue ethics can be more helpful if we could get a handle on those effects.

Relational ethics

Drawing either from a spiritual sense of connectedness between persons and/or aspects of largely female experiences of connectedness, various philosophers across a broad spectrum focus on caring relations as the basis for ethics. There is much variation in this ethical tradition, but the relatively recent caring tradition has been very influential in educational thought. Examples are found in Martin Buber (1958/1923) and Nel Noddings (1984, 1992). The emphasis is on the quality of the relation between the ethical actor and the receiver of the ethical action. Beyond that, the differences within the tradition can be quite dramatic. In Buber's terms, the relation is between I and Thou, a relation marked by the respect for the Thou's complete humanity, as opposed to a subject–object relation between I and "it." In Noddings' ethic, the relation is between the one-caring and the cared-for, characterized by the one-caring's engrossment in the needs of the cared-for and the one-caring's motivational displacement, helping the cared-for achieve his or her project.

When explained in spiritual terms, relational ethics is often criticized for its religious trappings, and critics may reasonably question its applicability among nonbelievers or in secular settings such as public schools, where multiple spiritual traditions are represented and deserve to be respected. When it draws from women's experience, the caring tradition is criticized on one hand, for essentializing Western white middle-class women's experiences of mothering as an ethic, and on the other hand, for confounding ethics with emotional experience that cannot be universalized. A relational ethic may come across as so intense that it is difficult to enact, and Noddings for one has been clear to argue that the one-caring should not be all sacrificing, but critics sometimes argue that the one-caring pays a high toll for caring so intently. As an ethic based on a caring relation, it is less clear how to enact social ethics and responsibilities to others outside the caring relation.

Since the initial publication of Noddings' first book on caring in 1984, educational scholars have found her ethic of caring to be a promising alternative to traditional ethics, especially among feminists and critical theorists, and the theory has influenced teaching and leadership scholarship as well. Educators who read the work find it a compelling way to alter their thinking about ethics, away from a theory of imposition to a more natural and nurturing form of ethics. The ethic of caring can help teachers who position themselves as committed to their students, and it can provide them with a way to think of day-to-day relations with others in their holistic qualities. A relational ethics reminds educators of the importance of situations and contexts, but in a less calculating manner than in consequentialist ethics. As an ethic built on the experience of natural caring, educators can draw on the most important ethical relations in their lives and displace their own motivations when relating with others.

The critiques of relational ethics may further help educators to avoid the tendency to lose themselves in caring. Noddings (1984) speaks of the important ways in which a cared-for completes the relation through gratitude and acceptance of caring. While students find it applicable to individual practice, they find it more difficult to imagine a whole school built around caring relations because it requires a different orientation toward educational practice, as Noddings (1992) explains. Recently, my graduate students have remarked that adapting an ethic of caring to their practice depends to a great extent on a school's context and culture, with test-driven school settings seemingly less amenable to a caring ethics.

At Sid's school, a relational ethic might help us see the various ethical situations in a new light. If we take Noddings' ethic of caring as a guide, we could position Sid as a one-caring who has various cared-fors in his proximity—his teachers and his students, and we could extend that also to include his family and his community. As one-caring, we would expect him to exhibit engrossment and motivational displacement. We would look for him to become engrossed in the needs and goals of his students and work within his power to ensure that their educational experience helps them meet their needs and achieve their goals; we would expect him to place their needs above his. Similarly we could position him as also concerned with the teachers' needs. Sid's willingness to displace his authority in deference to their discomfort with the chanting curriculum could be an indication of acting as one-caring, for in this example he rejects an abstract principle of obedience and encourages his teachers to do the same. If we were to characterize him as a principal who is one-caring, we would provide ethical heft to the slogan often heard that "we need to do what's best for the kids." This ethic would provide a primary rationale for rethinking how he responds to the comment from the anonymous superior that "the principalship was not a platform to be able to dispute these things," providing him an ethical stance for acting, rather than perhaps an oppositional stance. It remains an open question to what extent enacting an ethic of caring in a high-stakes situation can keep sanctions from being enacted upon him, his teachers, his students, and his community. Sid is in spirit and disposition very much like principals of other schools in the area who do not have nearly the challenge enacting an ethic of caring at a well-positioned school or a private, university-based laboratory school.

Post-structural ethics

Building from numerous critiques about the limitations of modern ethics, postmodern and post-structural ethics (the latter term seems more accurate as time goes on) offer alternative theories of how we encounter others. Insights are drawn from the critique of the modern self as assumed to be a sovereign, innocent, and knowing moral actor (Blake et al., 1998). Examples are found throughout the scholarship, building from multiple trajectories instigated by existentialist and Continental structuralist thought. Influential theorists include Jacques Derrida, Michel Foucault, and Emmanuel Levinas, and each have inspired ethical theory in education (Biesta, 2006; Todd, 2004). The ethical theory is varied, as a result, with a commonality the quest for an ethics without assurances of certainty. A post-structural ethic of risk, solidarity, and difference by Sharon Welch (1990) is a vital and compelling early articulation of Foucault's (and others') early work. Welch builds an ethic from the history of African American struggle for civil rights and embeds a critique of Western themes of control. Foucault's work on disciplinary power, surveillance, and care of the self has informed the work of many scholars and informs my own framework in this book, as I discuss more fully in subsequent chapters.

While some lesser known works like Welch's make robust ethics out of post-structural theory, and by now significant work is being done in education to make use of post-structural work in critical and emancipatory ethical projects, one of the most common criticisms is that these ethical theories are critiques of ethics only and provide justification only for inaction. Other criticisms are that the ethical content provides incomprehensible guidance to the ethical actor, or that these theories provide neither guidance nor hope for social ethics.

Educators have much to gain from engaging post-structural ethics. Some post-structural ethics address how power relations work in postmodern spaces and have the potential to help educators think differently about the circumstances in which they find themselves. It also has the potential for providing additional frames of relations between the self and other. In their aptly titled book, *Thinking Again: Education After Postmodernism,* Nigel Blake, Paul Smeyers, Richard Smith, and Paul Standish (1989) argue that the push to consider postmodern ethics as nihilistic is misplaced, and that education scholarship should make use of the insights of post-structural theory to help illuminate the ethical challenges associated with educational phenomena. From the critiques, however, educators can be advised that initial forays into post-structural theory could leave them with the distinct impression that there is no manner in which they may truly act ethically. The challenge is getting beyond the quest for certain outcomes and risking an ethic that may open possibilities that are not otherwise obvious.

The seeming absurdity of Sid's situation at his school could be explained fruitfully with a post-structural theoretical frame. It could also illustrate the nihilistic tendencies that post-structural theory is criticized for encouraging. And so, as with the other ethical traditions, this reflection will take the form of suitability and unanswered questions. To take Foucault as an example (and as a preview of what is to come in the following chapters), Sid has already used some of the post-structural language in his depiction of PSSA and PVAAS testing as governmental surveillance, with the implication that through these testing systems, the state is poised to control the actions of the principals and teachers. There is ample evidence in this story that this control is happening, and the ways in which it is happening is straight out of Foucault: teachers are effectively disciplining themselves, placing themselves under the surveillance of the state, teaching a curriculum that they do not like, because (as Sid believes) they are afraid of the consequences if they do not. They discipline themselves even though Sid (their direct supervisor) tells them they need not. From the story, we do not know who encouraged them to use the chanting curriculum. The seeming anonymity of that missing force may be accidental (with more information, we might find out it is part of a power struggle between Sid and the curriculum director), but in any event, the unnamed force makes a good point: often the vague and impersonal threat of punishment is more effective than a direct personal threat at encouraging people to discipline themselves.

Although the example fits neatly Foucault's theory of disciplinary power, we are still left to ponder how Sid and his teachers may act ethically in this situation. Rather than coming to a premature closure, I instead offer some key questions (problematics) that a post-structural ethics would do well to address. Namely:

- How might Sid help his teachers more effectively see how they have the opportunity to rethink their reluctance to resist the chanting curriculum?
- How might Sid come to understand what is behind teachers' trepidation to follow their better judgment?
- If part of the teachers' trepidation is emotional, how can they draw on ethics that may emotionally support them acting on their better judgment?
- How might the curriculum director question how the district's own practices (particularly the ones the district is freely implementing because it is focused on compliance) work against its better judgment about what is worthwhile for students to do and learn?
- How might Sid help his teachers rethink the role that the six children play in the philosophy of education of the school? How might they use the example of these children to reframe their notion of responsibility?
- How might district leadership create conditions that encourage school leaders and teachers to innovate freely and avoid the dangers associated with the well-documented effects of high-stakes accountability policy, especially in school districts like this one that does not meet all of its accountability targets?

4

From accountability (for test results) to responsibility (for children)

A+, arts, and accountability

In 1995, 25 elementary, middle, and high schools in North Carolina began implementing an arts integration program that had them reorganizing their curriculum around art, music, dance, and drama; implementing thematic units across grade levels; and studying Howard Gardner's theory of multiple intelligences. These 25 schools became the first participants in the A+ Schools Network, a school reform network that in 2011 has grown to include 45 schools in North Carolina, 68 schools in Oklahoma, and a professional development program that serves schools in Arkansas.

For the most part, the first 25 North Carolina schools had a good first year. Despite some drama that came from a last-minute cut in funding from the state legislature, the schools began experimenting with the features of the program—what came to be known as the A+ essentials: arts instruction and integration, thematic curriculum, experiential learning, multiple intelligences theory, collaboration, climate, infrastructure, and enriched assessment. For many of the schools, A+ was a tremendous opportunity to ramp up the quality of their instruction. It provided them focus, an expanded arts curriculum, and access to professional development. Researchers in the first year found eager and very diverse school sites, including two urban arts magnets, a rural "discovery" magnet, a tiny K-6 mountain-top school with four teachers, and a K-12 school nestled in the mountains that started a high-school conga band; most of the rest were moderate- to high-poverty elementary schools in urban and rural locations. Schools started slowly, energized by the ideas they had learned about, but by the end of the year still learning how to enact them all systematically.

Then came high-stakes accountability in the form of North Carolina's high-stakes testing program, one of the precursors to NCLB. In the summer of 1996, the state named about half of its schools low-performing, including about half of the A+ Schools (the state did what Noddings [2007] notes became prevalent after NCLB, using previous average scores to set grade-level proficiency; as a result, it was not surprising that about half the schools would score below average). The effect of labeling schools was immediate and palpable. Across the state, schools spent the next year scrambling to prepare students for better test performance. The next year, only about 15 percent of the state's schools failed to meet their performance targets, and that number was somewhat less for the A+ Schools.

Inside A+ Schools, the difference between Year 1 and Year 2 was dramatic. In some schools, especially those named low-performing, test preparation began to crowd out arts integration, and weekly dance and drama instruction began to fade. The research team collected data about how morbid many of the previously energized schools had become (Groves, 2002), with a large group of the low-performing schools settled into maintaining their engagement with A+ minimally, continuing to affiliate with the program, but without discernable capacity building around the A+ essentials. In some cases, accountability pressures delayed, complicated, or derailed efforts to implement the A+ Program (Gordon, 2002; Groves, 2002; Gunzenhauser & Gerstl-Pepin, 2002; McKinney, 2002; Murillo & Flores, 2002; Patterson, 2002). But those that affiliated most closely with the eight essentials associated with the A+ Program achieved in the state's accountability system, for the most part using the eight essentials as engaging educational ideas (Noblit et al., 2009). For schools able to innovate using the A+ essentials, "the A+ Schools Program offered teachers the opportunity to become more intentional about teaching the state curriculum, to teach holistically, and to collaborate across the school" (Gunzenhauser & Noblit, 2011, p. 435).

When Oklahoma began its A+ Schools in 2002, coincidentally, the same thing happened. NCLB's requirements kicked in, and Oklahoma, which had limited experience with standards beforehand and had only recently begun statewide testing, instituted its federally mandated high-stakes accountability program, naming low-performing schools at the end of Year 1 of A+. The difference in the A+ Schools between Year 1 and Year 2 was a little less dramatic in Oklahoma, partly because few schools were able to afford dance or drama instruction, and none of the Oklahoma schools initially had all four art forms represented in their weekly schedules. Also, many of the Oklahoma schools were at the same time also implementing Core Knowledge, Great Expectations, and scripted reading and/or mathematics curricula. For few of the Oklahoma schools in the first years A+ was an organizing theme.

It both states, it was about the time of Year 3 of their A+ Programs that things started to turn around for some of the low-performing schools. In North Carolina in Year 3, two-time low-performing schools were facing the possibility of sanctions if they remained in that category for a third year, so innovation-by-fire kicked in at some schools. The research team eventually concluded that in these early years, the schools fell into three categories, depending on the extent to which they engaged with the A+ essentials. The team found that schools which substantively engaged with the A+ essentials, regardless of their initial status in the accountability program, achieved recognition status by the end of the 4-year study. The research team surmised that the A+ essentials and the professional development enabled schools to build their capacity around arts integration, cultivate their internal accountability (Carnoy et al., 2003), and in doing so, meet the demands of external accountability (Gunzenhauser & Noblit, 2011).

Some of the capacity-building approaches were novel, unexpected, and contradictory. The most drastic example was at Creekside Elementary, where the school's two-time, low-performing label had already made it easier for the superintendent in the large, county-wide district to allocate additional resources to Creekside, a school without a powerful parent base. Creekside enrolled a mix of children from settled lower-middle income families and a transitional population of children from lower income and occasionally homeless families (despite an annual turnover rate that approached 50%, when we returned in fourth grade to interview children we had observed as first graders, nearly all the children were still at the school).

The principal at Creekside decided in the middle of Year 3 that weekly instruction in the four art forms, two-way arts integration, and thematic instruction across the curriculum were neither working nor making the best use of the arts specialists in the building. She was somewhat correct in that the program was not working very well, with a large number of new and inexperienced teachers who knew little about A+. The principal had adopted a policy teachers called "90/90/60," in which instruction each day encompassed 90 minutes of reading, 90 minutes of math, and 60 minutes of writing (Gunzenhauser & Noblit, 2001). Other subjects, including science, social studies, physical education, and the four arts vied for the remaining time in the school day. She decided at mid-year to enact an arts-infused math curriculum to make use of the arts specialists and their art forms in service to math achievement, the area that had been most difficult for the school to find improvement. She partnered the arts specialists with grade-level teachers in the tested grades of third, fourth, and fifth grade. With two adults in the room for math, and occasional team teaching and arts integration, discipline referrals in those classrooms dropped precipitously, and Creekside's math scores improved. The school eventually lost its "low-performing" label, but large portions of the state curriculum were left untaught to students in tested grades.

While in both states, the A+ Program predated high-stakes accountability, a constant concern of teachers and principals in the network are performance on standardized tests and resulting effects on a school's categorization. To its credit, the A+ Network never promised to raise schools' test scores; it instead encourages teachers to integrate (thematically and collaboratively) a rich, comprehensive curriculum that addresses the state standards and includes the arts. The goals of integrating the arts and assessing student learning often come into conflict when achievement is defined narrowly by performance on standardized measures and when the state and districts increase their control over professional development, curriculum, and instruction.

Prior to engaging in A+, the language of philosophy often failed these educators. It is not clear that all of them even believed in the efficacy of the test scores, but few conveyed language to counteract testing pressures or even to talk about it any differently. Educators participating substantively in the A+ Programs in North Carolina and Oklahoma eventually found a different language to talk about success. Teachers in North Carolina early on realized that they needed some form of alternative or enriched assessment to capture the value of the educational ideas that they were trying to enact (assessment, enriched or otherwise, was not a component of the original professional development agenda). It is an ongoing process to develop a rich language that others find understandable and compelling.

Both states' A+ Networks owe their remarkable sustainability and persistence to a double accomplishment: the teachers are so convinced philosophically by the A+ essentials that they remain willing to be engaged up to 16 years later; second, the policy makers in both states seem satisfied with the test scores that the A+ Schools produce in largely high-needs areas. The schools involved tend to outperform other schools in the state and other schools in their districts on standardized test measures, even though the student populations in their schools tend to have lower SES and higher percentages of minority populations than average. None of the research attempted or desired to attribute cause and effect to these relations, and claims made in print are descriptive rather than inferential. However, the evidence is strong enough for policy makers, who understand causality not as a scientific construct but as a discursive construct.

Philosophically, because schools apply to participate in A+ out of their interest in arts integration and the other A+ essentials, they become engaged modestly at first and then can grow over time in their ability to collaborate, integrate, and innovate around thematic instruction and arts integration (Noblit et al., 2009; Raiber et al., 2010). Through the A+ essentials and ongoing professional development, participation in the A+ Program gave schools the opportunity to take responsibility for students and their holistic education (Gunzenhauser & Noblit, 2011).

Accountability or responsibility?

The story of the A+ Network in North Carolina and Oklahoma presents schools under the threat of high-stakes accountability using their participation in an initiative rich in educational ideas to find a route toward improvement that does not leave them accepting a default philosophy of education that relies on teaching to the test. For many schools, A+ provides a substantive alternative that provides a method for engaging the standards (in Oklahoma) or standards-based curriculum (in North Carolina). It has effectively provided schools with a way to exercise responsibility for students instead of mere accountability for test scores.

In this chapter I argue for an alternative conception of "accountability" in the form of a more meaningful and sustainable concept, "responsibility." Responsibility provides a stronger platform upon which to articulate a professional ethics. I argue that a notion of responsibility may form the basis for shifting the discourse about accountability in a direction that promotes professionalism as a concept that acknowledges the difficulties that teachers face enacting responsibility, when accountability is called for. Several philosophers of education have also argued for a move from accountability to responsibility, including Gert Biesta, Nel Noddings, and Ken Sirotnik. In educational policy, Richard Elmore and his coauthors have addressed similar issues, and in educational leadership, Robert Starratt and Thomas Sergiovanni have argued for educational practice that is likewise organized around responsibility.

One approach that I could take is to suggest a more responsible accountability system, which first of all, takes greater responsibility and care for its use of statistical measures, and second, which expands the focus on who is responsible for public education to lawmakers, policy makers, and communities (Oakes et al., 2004; Ravitch, 2010; Sirotnik, 2004). Suggested features of a more responsible accountability system would include setting higher standards for all children, funding education more equitably, incorporating professional development for building capacity, and using testing in a manner that is technically more appropriate. Additionally, critics have argued that a more responsible accountability system would need to address the disproportionate amount of resources that have been diverted to private entities that provide products and services designed to help schools raise test scores, but which have questionable educational merit (Sunderman et al., 2005).

Although making an accountability system more responsible is something I would encourage, that is not my approach here, because I am not focused at the moment on how to change the policy. Also, I am not confident that any accountability system that is primarily externally imposed would lead to higher quality education across the board, because the logic of rewards and sanctions for student achievement is fundamentally flawed. The threat of sanctions, in particular, encourages unethical practices, because it encourages teachers and school leaders to think about themselves first and their students for their value in helping them make themselves look better. When test scores are considered to be unachievable (such is the case with many students who are English language learners or who qualify for special education), the temptation is great to avoid taking responsibility for the education of those students. The promise for receiving rewards can be perceived as a threat of sanction all the same; if I am the only one of my colleagues who does not receive a reward, I can rather easily interpret that state of affairs as my receiving a sanction, particularly if in a given year, the reward is my only chance for a salary increase, while meanwhile costs for health insurance and day care are rising. For all of these reasons, rewards and sanctions make responsibility more difficult, not less.

My approach instead is to focus on responsibility and build a notion of professionalism upon it. As several others have done, I call for renewed attention to ethical considerations in day-to-day practice, mindful of the external demands, social pressures, and power relations that influence the educational process. In day-to-day practice, the relation between the teacher and the student is primary, and so we need a notion of professionalism that addresses that primary relation. Unfortunately, in education, we lack a popular language of professional responsibility for all children, and we need one to go up against the very powerful language of accountability. We also lack a popular language of relation between the teacher and student that would remind us of its importance in the educational experience, and we need one of these also to go up against the pressure to treat children as test scores. To make this argument, I draw from recent work that names the conceptual and material dangers associated with the concept of "accountability."

What is the primary relation in accountability?

In writing about school accountability policy in the United Kingdom, philosopher Gert Biesta (2004) argues that in order to work, accountability policy relies upon two related but distinct notions. First, it requires accountability for test scores and, second, a notion of responsibility for children. In my research work, I have found that the latter is what draws educators into the logic of accountability policy. Educators, for the most part, believe themselves to be responsible for the education of children, and indeed, many or most educators are drawn to education because of that responsibility. One might also argue that a teacher's notion of responsibility toward children is an important component of an educator's philosophy of education. We should call this form of responsibility *professional responsibility*.

As Biesta (2004) helps us to see, an important difference between accountability and responsibility is the relation that is of primary importance. For educators who believe firmly in their professional responsibility for children, the most significant relation is between the teacher and the student. This is a relation of responsibility that teachers believe they know, it is a relation over which they believe they have some control, and it is a relation which they believe needs to be protected. This is a good starting point for teachers (and for those who are preparing themselves to be teachers).

In the logic of accountability policy, Biesta (2004) argues that the most significant relation is instead between the "state" and the "school." One needs only to look carefully at how accountability policy is structured to see how this plays out. NCLB mandates that states put in place accountability systems that measure at the school level how well they are able to educate students as measured by standardized measurements of achievement.

When an accountability system is based upon school-level measures of accountability, the underlying logic is that educators will be motivated to do a better job of serving children (and all children, not just the ones they might normally focus on) if the school in which the educators work must produce adequate test score gains in order to avoid a sanction of some sort and/or to receive a reward. The school is "made to be accountable" for its results, and in the passive voice of the phrase "is made to be accountable," the identity of the person, institution, or entity to which the school is accountable is hidden, as is the entity that makes the school accountable. To whom is the school accountable? To the governor? To parents? To taxpayers? We might answer that the missing object is the "state," and that could be correct, for the state establishes the system of accountability, so we have a relationship here between the school and the state.

As Biesta (2004) argues, accountability policy makes this relationship primary. The amorphous nature of both of these concepts, "school" and "state," is somewhat of a problem at face value, because neither is a specific person. It is not correct to say that the principal, for instance, is responsible to the state secretary of education. While it may be true that a principal's job could be on the line if test scores do not improve, there is no guarantee that this is the case (the principal could find another job and escape a sanction assigned to a school, and in any event, the law is not written such that the state secretary would do the firing). In other words, the most important relationship in this structure is between two entities, and all of the personal relationships which I have identified are secondary to that relationship.

That this is the case—that the relation between the school and the state is more important than the relation between the teacher and the student—is evident in the number of unintended outcomes that arise from accountability policy. Educational practices that are more concerned with raising the test scores of the school, such as focusing on "bubble kids" or coordinated cheating, serve this vague relation between the school and the state. These and other observed phenomena discussed in Chapter 2 have been referred to as "unintended consequences" of accountability policy. They are consequences nonetheless of relocating the most important relation away from the student and teacher.

The shift in the primacy of relation is a major ethical problem. When de-emphasized, the teacher–student relation is subject to multiple pressures and is fundamentally altered. And on top of that, the teacher–student relation is only one of the important relations that are made subservient to the school–state relation. Accountability policy, in other words, disrupts the significant relationships involved in public education. As such, accountability policy disrupts the central relation for ethical activity in schools.

The rise of accountability

The language of "accountability" has a well-documented history, and as some have argued, the concept's growing importance in education has identifiable historical markers in the recent past. In the last 50 years in federal education policy, there were two important moments that altered how public schools had traditionally been responsible to the public (Cuban, 2004; Oakes et al., 2004). Prior to 1965, accountability could more accurately be described as responsibility, because school board members were the ones held responsible for the quality of education in their districts. Local accountability came in the form of elections, and there was little need for accountability beyond that level. As Larry Cuban (2004) explains, the first important turning point in public school accountability occurred in 1965, when the US Congress authorized the initial Elementary and Secondary Education Act (ESEA), which provided federal dollars so that states could improve the differential educational experiences of children living in poverty and children in minority racial and ethnic groups. To address concern that the money be spent wisely and for its intended purpose, ESEA included accountability provisions, so that states would be accountable to the federal government for how those dollars were spent (Oakes et al., 2004).

The second important turning point was the 1989 governors' educational summit, which set a three-part federal agenda for higher standards, greater accountability, and increased resources. As Jeannie Oakes, Gary Blasi and John Rogers (2004) explain, the cost of following through on this agenda was deemed too expensive, and so the agenda for "increased resources" was replaced with a market competition rhetoric. Market advocates proposed competition for students between public schools and with charter schools as a financial alternative, drawing together multiple purposes to support the accountability movement. A fundamental issue with this development, Oakes et al. argue, is that the market rhetoric excused lawmakers from fundamental responsibility for policy and resources.

As Ravitch (2010) tells it, the push for higher standards was kept alive by forestalling the move for national educational standards and allowing states to develop their own standards. In 1994, Lynne Cheney went public with her criticism of the unreleased voluntary national history standards, which had yet to be fully vetted. Cheney attacked them as ideologically driven and hopelessly leftist in their political orientation. Despite Ravitch's argument at the time that the standards were a reasonable first draft and should be revised, Cheney's opportune attack led to an uproar. A culture war debate ensued over the control of the curriculum, the history standards became politically toxic, and the development of national standards became a "radioactive" policy issue (Ravitch, 2010). In the ensuing policy vacuum, the policy shift was to state-level standards. As Ravitch argues, the controversy over the history standards led to tepid state-level standards.

During the 1990s several states attempted high-stakes accountability systems to enforce standards-based reforms. California, Florida, Kentucky, Maryland, New York, North Carolina, and Texas were among the first generation of states to implement standards-based reform (Mintrop & Trujillo, 2005). States reported gains in student achievement as a result of their accountability systems, and federal policy in NCLB was modeled after the reported successes in these states. Subsequent research concluded that the first-generation states' reported improvements were limited to state measures, and those effects did not appear on the National Assessment of Educational Progress (NAEP):

> The results imply that the first-generation accountability states with high-stakes testing policies in place prior to NCLB have adopted relatively lower performance standards, leading to overestimation of their proficiency rates and underestimation of the achievement gap. The findings also suggest that policy-makers become more aware of potential biases resulting from relying exclusively on states' own test measure for accountability. (Lee, 2006, p. 57)

Some of the research about first-generation states' experience with high-stakes accountability policy was published before NCLB was law, but the most substantive analysis was published afterward. This and other early research suggested that the high stakes attached to the testing regimens was already leading to effects contrary to the intention of the law. Sanctions in first-generation states were sporadically applied and did little to develop the capacity of schools that were deemed low-performing (Mintrop & Trujillo, 2005).

More responsible accountability

As NCLB unfolded, several educational researchers and theorists stepped forward to argue for a more responsible accountability system. In laying out the structure of his edited volume, Sirotnik (2004) is especially concerned with reframing conversations about accountability around responsible accountability as a way of *Holding Accountability Accountable,* the title of the book. Sirotnik is interested in expanding the notion of who should be accountable for public education. Not just teachers and principals, he argues, but also policy makers and elected officials should be accountable for the quality of public education. As Oakes et al. (2004) describe in that volume, lawmakers are not part of an accountability system and yet they are fundamentally responsible for the allocation of resources to implement the dual policies of high-stakes accountability systems—high standards and accountability for results.

Oakes et al. (2004) want greater responsibility in accountability to include attention to adequate resources, including updated textbooks, high-quality teachers (both in terms of preparation and ongoing professional development), and support services for children and families. Citing the tremendous variation in public school problems and issues and noting that schools that serve poor and minority populations are the most severely underserved, Oakes et al. argue that accountability should be an issue of neglect (understood broadly), rather than teacher motivation. As they say, "Good teaching requires more than motivation and effort. If the teacher lacks knowledge and skills, commitment alone will be a disservice to students" (p. 89). This view of responsible accountability is similar to the approach taken by others who are advocates of high-standards educational reform, but decry the overemphasis on high-stakes testing (Thompson, 2001). Among these authors are those who advocate a distinction between external and internal accountability (Carnoy et al., 2003).

Responsibility is a suitable replacement for accountability to begin a conversation about educational policy and practice. As Noddings (2007) argues, "in teaching, as in parenting, responsibility is the fundamental concept on which any reasonable concept of accountability must be built" (p. 38). The literature on accountability diverges depending on where policy makers and educational researchers stand on the relative importance of responsibility and accountability. Quite often the distinction is facile, merely a name change. But as Noddings argues: "Responsibility is a much deeper, wider ranging concept than accountability. . . . Teachers may be *accountable* to administrators for certain outcomes, but they are *responsible* to their students for a host of outcomes" (p. 39). The overemphasis of accountability at the expense of responsibility, she argues, is a holdover from appropriating the concept of accountability from business, on the logic of the bottom line, which translates poorly from business to education.

The downward push from administrators to be accountable competes with teachers' responsibility to their students. A fundamental conceptual problem arises, then, if accountability to those above is not "aligned" with responsibility to students (I am not arguing for yet another aspect of education that must be aligned). If actions to raise scores are not the same actions that enable teachers to enact their responsibility to students, there is the potential for conflict. If the actions work in the opposite direction, the situation is hopelessly dysfunctional. In schools under pressure to raise test scores, this has happened. When North Carolina began its accountability program in 1995, "accountability" was a very powerful term; when teachers heard the term, they were taken in, because they understood it as "responsibility" and had a hard time seeing accountability as anything but responsibility. Many teacher and administrator comments began, "I'm all for accountability, but. . ." What followed the "but" varied, but it was not until much later that the conflict between accountability and responsibility would be clear.

Despite the evidence that high-stakes accountability systems were not by themselves able to increase capacity in the low-performing schools in first-generation accountability states, "accountability" was still a very powerful term when the rest of the states had to develop accountability systems. Teachers generally do not wish to resist authority. So no sophisticated manipulation needed to be applied to them to get them to buy into accountability policies, because teachers do in fact feel morally responsible for the children under their care, and being disobedient to authority would not occur to most teachers as a responsible thing to do. However, this relational responsibility is the very nature of the student/teacher relation and what could be the basis for systematic improvement of educational experiences.

Economic accountability

The market metaphor that is so much a part of accountability policy has come under significant criticism from educational researchers and theorists concerned that accountability has changed the nature of relationships between schools and families. Among them are Gert Biesta (2004), Deron Boyles (2005), Sharon Gewirtz (2001), David Hursh (2007), Alex Molnar (2005), Trevor Norris (2011), Diane Ravitch (2010), and Ken Saltman (2007, 2010). Together, these authors have advanced arguments that direct us to pay closer attention to the kinds of relations that are fostered by an accountability system. Some argue that accountability systems are mirroring other recent developments in the relation between business and public education, wherein business interests encourage the development of children predominantly as consumers of products and services, both in the present and future (Boyles, 2005; Hursh, 2007; Norris, 2011; Saltman, 2010). An economy built upon mass consumption needs consumers willing to take their place in the chain of consumption, and so opportunities to build brand loyalty and consumption habits are valuable to corporations.

Ravitch (2010) is on to something quite similar and states it plainly: "Business leaders like the idea of turning the schools into a marketplace where the consumer is king. But the problem with the marketplace is that it dissolves communities and replaces them with consumers" (p. 221). She then asserts that "Education is too important to relinquish to the vagaries of the market and the good intentions of amateurs" (p. 222). A related criticism is how many resources go into test preparation. Accountability policy is quite expensive, because it leads to public dollars going toward associated educational industries (too large now to be called cottage industries) that supply tests, test preparation materials, tutoring services, motivational products, and other products that schools and districts purchase in attempts to raise scores (Sunderman et al., 2005).

There is another important sense in which schools and families can be said to be involved in economic relations. With school choice as a cornerstone of high-stakes accountability policy (and its place of prominence after significant resources were not forthcoming to fully fund a national program of high standards), it works to influence relations between families and schools and more particularly, between educators and students. This particular kind of economic relation relates directly to my emphasis on the student–teacher relation as a focus for educator professionalism, and in what follows, I draw from Biesta (2004) to explain why the demand for an economic relation between educators and students presents a profound ethical problem.

Biesta (2004) distinguishes between "economic accountability" and "political responsibility." Economic accountability derives from the logic of market choices. The logic of the market has a surface democratic appeal, Biesta acknowledges, the result of conflation of school choice with an exercise of democratic action: "'choice' is about the behavior of consumers in a market where their aim is to satisfy their needs; it should not be conflated with democracy, which is about public deliberation and contestation regarding the common good" (p. 237). School choice is not a democratic action, but an economic choice, an individualistic choice.

This distinction recalls Greene's (1988) concerns about the difficulties of educating for freedom in an individualistic society such as the United States: "How, in a society like ours, a society of contesting interests and submerged voices, an individualist society, a society still lacking an 'in-between,' can we educate for freedom?" (p. 116). Adopting the rhetoric of the market, the public school becomes a site for competing interests, replaying and amplifying the already present contestation of interests that have driven the hidden curriculum since the founding of public schools. As Gewirtz (2001) explains, "In education, parents are now seen as consumers and schools as small businesses, their income dependent on their success in attracting customers within competitive local markets" (p. i). The contestation of interests is itself not inherently oppressive. Instead, the conditions and grounds upon which that contestation plays out make it oppressive.

High-stakes accountability policy changes the conditions and grounds for how parents choose schools for their children. This change in education is part of broader changes in how relationships are fostered between consumers and states:

> One of the most significant results of this development—and recognizing this is essential to understanding the current mode of accountability in education—is the reconfiguration of the relationship between the state and its citizens. This relationship has become less a political relationship—that is, a relationship between government and citizens who, together, are concerned about the common good—and more an economic relationship—that is, a relationship between the state as provider and the taxpayer as consumer of public services (most significantly, health care, education, and social and economic security and safety). (Biesta, 2004, p. 237)

In this new arrangement, the easiest role available to a parent or student is the role as consumer of educational services (Biesta, 2004). Because educational accountability is conceptualized in economic terms (since the federal and state governments demand accountability for dollars spent on education), accountability is not to citizens or parents but to governmental agencies (or to the abstract "taxpayer," if you will). Biesta puts it this way:

> The core problem is that while many would want the culture of accountability to emphasize accountability to the public, it actually creates a system focused on accountability to regulators and the like, thereby removing the real stakeholders from the "accountability loop." (p. 240)

This relationship tends to work both ways: not only are parents positioned as shoppers for educational products, but schools who are held accountable for their students' test scores are now authorized to shop for students (Biesta, 2004). Biesta is concerned with what democratic aims may be reclaimed from moves toward accountability. Ultimately he decides that since accountability so fundamentally alters the relationship between the school and the student (and that relationship is so far from a notion of accountability as responsibility), the democratic potential of accountability cannot be regained.

Biesta (2004) arrives at this conclusion through use of Zygmunt Bauman's moral theory, in which nonreciprocal moral relationships (such as those between teacher and student) arise from the interaction between two persons in proximity. The pedagogical relation is a rather significant human relation, particularly since it is nonreciprocal. In other words, it is an unequal human relation in the very significant sense that the teacher is responsible for the student, but the student is not responsible for the teacher. High-stakes accountability policy can be said to rely on students' responsibility for the adults at their school, because the adults' livelihoods are at least somewhat dependent upon the students' performance on tests. Using this frame, it should be clear that this is an inappropriate moral relation.

A moral relationship is compromised when a third party intervenes, because it breaches the "one-to-one responsibility for the Other" (Biesta, 2004, p. 245), the proximal nature of moral relations, an aspect of the human condition. For Bauman, socialization processes alter moral impulses, and in the educational context, Biesta argues that they contribute to educators' opting out of responsibility. The third party gets in the way of the moral relationship, which Biesta argues is what accountability policy has rather effectively done. Biesta argues that accountability policy alters teachers' moral impulses, which makes it easier for them to think of themselves as providers of an educational service rather than as responsible for others:

> They have been maneuvered into a position in which it is easier to think of their relationship in economic terms as well. In using the term "easier," I am avoiding the suggestion that the "providers" and "consumers" have been pressed into this kind of thinking. The mechanisms at work are subtler and have more to do with falling into what turns out to be the most "convenient," most "normal" way of thinking and acting. Going against the grain always requires more effort and conviction than choosing the path of least resistance. (p. 248)

Educators need to understand the ways in which power works in this kind of discourse, so that they might understand why it seems so difficult to go against the grain to avoid falling into consumerist relations.

A similar difficulty arises for parents and students. In a reconfiguration of the relationship between public institutions and the public, the normal roles available to parents and students are roles as consumers of educational services. Parents shop for schools for their children. In areas like Allegheny County in Western Pennsylvania, where there are so many varied choices for elementary school, parents of preschool students continually engage each other in conversation about choosing a kindergarten program. In conversation, parents position themselves as consumers of educational services, and in only rare cases do they engage in discourse about how the patchwork of schooling options serve the common good. We lack (or lack experience using) a language about how our local public schools serve the common welfare of all students. The danger of collective action by parents is that they may band together around common but narrow interests that leave out children and parents who are not like them (Smith, 2004).

The difficulty of going against the grain is an example of how power works in high-stakes accountability policy. High stakes mean something to so many people (some fear the consequences, some do not want to be labeled as low-performing, some do not want to think of themselves as going against the grain, some just want to be normal). As high stakes they are difficult to ignore. People act in ways to try to influence desired outcomes, sometimes selfishly so they can keep their jobs, and sometimes because they truly believe that doing better on tests will provide their students with a better outcome (Mathison & Freeman, 2003). But as the literature on internal accountability has shown, quite often educators and educational institutions lack the capacity to actually improve their practice, so schools and teachers do what they can do, which may mean teaching to the test, narrowing the curriculum, or the numerous other documented practices that teachers, school leaders, testing coordinators, and curriculum directors have invented.

These insights make it clearer why schools do so many strange and unusual things in order to raise their school-wide test scores (such as focusing on "bubble kids"); it is in short "easier" to respond to the pressures of high-stakes accountability by addressing the measure to which a school is held accountable. As I mentioned earlier in this chapter, in Biesta's language, the more significant moral relation in this case has become the one between the school as an entity and the governing agency that is in charge of distributing rewards or sanctions. The primary relation is where accountability rules action. Meanwhile, teachers and students are tied into an economic relation that is secondary to this primary relation. This insight should also eliminate any lingering doubts we have that market choices have anything at all to do with democratic action. Market choices are about individuals seeking to satisfy individual needs.

The vague nature of this relation between the impersonal "school" and the even more impersonal "governing agency" would be merely a conceptual problem, if it did not actually make the relation more effective. In other words, this is not a precise moral relation between two persons in any conventional sense. Even if there are two actual persons at stake here—for instance, a teacher whose students' test scores are subpar and the superintendent deciding whether or not to fire the teacher for poor performance—the economic accountability model does not even make this particular relation primary. The superintendent's authorization for firing the teacher is the product of a more primary, generalized, and abstract relation—ultimately accountability to the *idea* of a governing agency.

Although the relation between the school and the state is vague in this sense, it is quite significant to the moral position of the teacher who relates to students and to the moral position of the superintendent who relates to teachers. As suggested in Sid's example at the opening of Chapter 3, the threat of sanction (or even the *possible* threat of a sanction) is a powerful motivator for action. It is easier in this situation for teachers to act in ways that avoid the sanction; to act otherwise is more difficult. While it seems to be quite difficult to act in other ways, educators need not claim a nihilistic stance about the impossibility of taking moral responsibility. Biesta and others argue instead that the difficulty of claiming moral responsibility points out its necessity and possibility. I have more to say about this important point in later chapters (it is an example of normalization [as described in Chapter 5] and the opportunity to care for the self [Chapter 6] and for resisting normalization [Chapter 7]).

The importance that high-stakes accountability policy awards to the relation between the school and the state does not necessarily mean that the relation between the school and its governing agency is now the most important moral site for resisting the dangers of high-stakes accountability policy. It is truly significant (and effective even) to suggest that political action to work against the dangers of accountability policy should focus on schools as collectives to band together in a plan of resistance. I am certainly all for that form of collective action (see Vinson & Ross, 2003). However, Biesta helps us to see more fundamentally that the pedagogical relation has been fundamentally damaged by accountability policy. It has lost not only the proximity essential to moral responsibility, but also the two other features Bauman describes—the exemption of certain others from consideration as appropriate recipients of moral responsibility and "disassembling the object of action into a set of 'traits,' so that it no longer appears as a (potentially) moral self" (Biesta, 2004, p. 246).

Biesta (2004) argues that accountability systems have all three of these features of dehumanization covered. This interpretation figures prominently in Biesta's conclusion about the possibility that accountability systems may retain their democratic appeal:

> Against this background I am inclined to conclude that the culture of accountability ultimately makes relationships of responsibility impossible. Accountability is not simply another discourse about how we might understand responsibility, nor is it just one more definition or operationalization of responsibility. The culture of accountability, driven as it is by economic relationships, poses a serious threat to the possibility for proximity. Bauman's account of the three ways in which the moral impulse can be neutralized—distance, the exemption of some others from the class of potential "objects" of responsibility, and disassembling others into "traits"—offers a surprisingly accurate account of the microrelationships that are brought about by the culture of accountability. In other words, it reveals that the technical–managerial approach to accountability can in no way be reconciled with an approach in which responsibility is central. (p. 250)

To reiterate from just above, this conclusion does not lead to a nihilistic vision for responding to the pressures of accountability. Biesta is addressing from a policy standpoint whether the push for accountability—enacted through test-based and competition-based systems—can regain its democratic potential. He concludes that the policy itself cannot be salvaged as a democratic project. We are, however, left with the conditions of the policy in which we must act as educators.

Other critics of high-stakes accountability policy are likewise concerned about the potential of an accountability system to achieve its goals. Among the dissenters, Ravitch (2010) argues that higher standards and smarter use of testing could save the accountability movement, but I am not optimistic. The high stakes associated with test score targets simply makes it too difficult for moral responsibility to survive and flourish. Short of changing policy (or in preparation for the next level of policy), we need a more robust moral language in education that provides guidance for making the teacher–student relation primary to our practice and that keeps us alert to the dangers associated with policies and procedures that work against the pedagogical relation as primary.

Responsibility through the arts

Returning now to the story of the A+ Schools, it is helpful to think of what the arts are supposed to help people to do: to see each other as differently oriented toward the creative. Engaging with the arts emphasizes that education is about becoming, not solely about acquiring knowledge (Greene, 1988). Because the arts present substantive educational ideas, engaging them works, and sustaining one's engagement with the arts continues to open up possibilities for one's practice, one's relations with students, and expansive experiences for children. The schools participating in the A+ Schools Program have an opportunity to create school cultures built around the arts, and the other seven essentials provide them a method for doing so. Learning about the essentials is a continuing process, with schools setting achievable goals each year. Because teachers in A+ Schools at the same time had to meet the requirements of the state's accountability system, they are called to either embrace the arts as a route to accountability or to consider it as something to the side (Gunzenhauser & Noblit, 2011; Raiber et al., 2010).

Schools which fully identified themselves with the A+ essentials provided themselves with a route for being successful with external accountability. Using Carnoy et al.'s (2003) language, these schools concentrated on their internal accountability. Arts-based schools can fall into the category of orthogonal schools, which means that they may not do well in external accountability. Because the A+ Schools were encouraged from the beginning to start with the state curriculum, they did not position themselves as orthogonal to the state accountability system. Instead, they developed themselves as internally accountable to their schools' individual adaptation of the A+ essentials. They did not allow the state's high-stakes testing to define their practice, an action that may have made them accountable to the state, but not responsible, for they would have had to defer to a default philosophy of education that valued test scores over learning, and the accumulation of narrow, tested knowledge and skills, over a full curriculum.

5

Normalization, surveillance, and the self-disciplined

Normalizing Sam

On professional days, Sam Galloway often arrives to school astride a black Harley–Davidson motorcycle. A tall, balding man with a neatly trimmed goatee, Sam strides with purpose and speaks in a creamy baritone. Confident, clear, and consistent, Sam leads a middle school in a suburban Pennsylvania school district that regularly scores highly on the state's tests—the PSSAs, named after the state's accountability program, the Pennsylvania System of School Assessment. I have known Sam for several years and visited his school in 2006 to see how high-stakes accountability policy had affected him and his teachers. He has been an educator for more than 25 years, and for more than a decade has been a middle-school principal.

During the summer, Sam receives visits from prospective parents, newcomers to the area considering the purchase of a home. They are considering various schools that have comparable test scores, and they visit individual schools to help them decide which subdivision in which to buy. There are multiple school districts of varying size in the area, and several districts in Sam's area are in communities with comparable housing stock, housing prices, and amenities. The communities are all comparable commuting distances from the downtown area.

Talking about these parent visits, Sam acknowledges that what he tells parents about his school is mediated by other influences—the offhand comments of real estate agents, the opinions of work colleagues, and particularly in this area, long-held beliefs about the relative quality of the various school districts in the community. He says it is a time to be a bit of a salesman. He is proud of his school and enjoys sharing it with parents considering moving into the community. These parents ask good questions, Sam says. They are mostly interested in curriculum and technological resources and are impressed with the online access his school provides to students' curriculum materials.

Sam describes how accountability causes pressure:

> The pressure mainly comes from the district, because they publish the scores in the paper and there is a lot of comparison in this area between [neighboring districts] and they seem to focus on that in the paper. . . . The parents go to school board meetings and ask why this building is 10 points higher than this building, and [they say] "maybe I should have bought my house in this area instead of over here." [Pause] It's not a huge problem. [Pause] But it's natural to want to do better.

The public display of test scores and Sam's opportunity to market his school to visiting parents are small parts of the larger high-stakes accountability system in Pennsylvania. They are evidence of the new kinds of arrangements between schools and parents that high-stakes accountability policy has fostered. Along with test scores, facilities, technology, curriculum offerings, and other factors, the school visits are additional ways in which schools can be said to compete for students with neighboring school districts.

Sam leads a middle school that is "well-positioned" to meet the demands of external accountability (Carnoy et al., 2003): it has a stable and experienced teaching faculty, it is well-funded, it has an updated physical plant, it has a low percentage of students who receive free- or reduced-price lunches (around 15%), it is largely white (about 98%), and as Sam describes it, the families have largely middle- and upper-middle incomes. Sam's school enrolls significant numbers of children who are already reading on grade level and do well on their tests. Teachers don't have to "teach to the test" in order for students to do well.

Sam believes that special test preparation is unnecessary: "I'm not one of those principals who shut down a month before the tests and eliminate specials. . . . I don't hold assemblies and all these kinds of incentives." Sam believes the value of education is that it enables children to become responsible for the world, both for personal decision making and civic responsibility. Sam's philosophy came out most clearly when he recounted the educational values he has stressed in his career:

> Whenever I would talk to my students as a teacher or a coach, I always thought that it was important for them to understand that it was their responsibility for making the world a better place. I always thought that

education was the key to that. . . . We're always talking to the students about their responsibility for contributing to society and being able to become informed so that they can make good decisions about things.

His school is not a "target school"; it is not the target of high-stakes accountability policy (Carnoy et al., 2003). Sam is not fully supportive of NCLB, but he sees some benefit in his school. He has used the opportunity of the push for external accountability to "blow out the cobwebs" in his school and to make teachers more responsible for their lesson plans and for working together to meet grade-level standards. The district uses textbooks that are keyed to state grade-level standards and to "anchors," the term that came into use in Pennsylvania after NCLB to denote tested content.

Because the curriculum materials align with the state standards, Sam is confident that his school will meet its proficiency targets in the PSSAs without any of the additional interventions that are replete in the research literature, such as narrowing the curriculum to tested subjects, making use of practice-testing, holding testing pep rallies, or attempting to exempt low-achieving children. Nor is there any need to engage in coordinated cheating. He encourages his teachers to avoid "teaching to the test," but pressure to do so comes from an unexpected source—his teachers, some of whom worry when they hear that other, competing districts have suspended instruction prior to testing and run practice tests with their students. The teachers worry they are not doing enough in Sam's school to maximize student test-score performance. Sam tells them that if they are following the standards all along, they have nothing to worry about. If they are suspending curriculum to do extra test preparation, it is not with his knowledge or support.

Throughout my collaborative research projects, I have heard a number of unexpected stories from educators about how high-stakes accountability has affected their beliefs and practices. The details from Sam's interview suggest some curious and subtle exercises of power—and by multiple people. Sam's school and district are not under siege; none of the schools in his district are in danger of being named low-performing by the state, qualifying for corrective action, or being taken over by the state. The state is not explicitly exercising power over the school. Instead, it happens more subtly through the actions of individuals and institutions.

Some exercises of power are expected and reflect the hierarchy of roles. As a leader, Sam takes the opportunity of accountability policy to encourage his teachers to work together to teach the same content. He works with his teachers to improve their lesson plans, to make their plans more explicit. The district selects textbooks and curriculum materials aligned with the standards. In another portion of the interview, Sam mentions how much easier his superintendent makes it to acquire resources for the middle school.

As more subtle exercises of power, parents take what is reported in the newspaper and make comments based on what they believe the scores mean (in this case, that a 10-point difference in scores means something significant about the differential quality of a school, but any meaning they make is an exercise of power). Sam exercises power when he has the opportunity to talk with visiting parents, giving them a chance to hear his educational ideas; he could even influence the way they make their decision, perhaps encouraging them to consider educational ideas rather than test scores. Sam exercises power when he uses the opportunity of external accountability to encourage teachers to be more intentional about their teaching. And most compelling is how his teachers attempt to discipline themselves and spend time doing what teachers at other schools do—set aside their lesson plans to give kids test practice (and it is important that we not demonize or diminish the integrity of this impulse, for the teachers may have their students' best interests in mind when they make this suggestion). Importantly, Sam discourages his teachers from suspending their curriculum to do test preparation, but some suspect they should. Sam sees alignment as the most defensible approach, and he does not want his teachers to acquiesce any more to the power of testing.

Foucault's theory of disciplinary power

This chapter is the first of three that draw from the work of Michel Foucault. In this chapter, I explain the fundamental ethical problem of high-stakes accountability policy: the danger of expanding the normalizing power of the examination into more aspects of educational practice. I wish to argue that normalization is at the center of the difficulties associated with changing practices and priorities in public education. Already one of the projects of modern institutions that make self-disciplined subjects, normalization has become an even more powerful project under high-stakes accountability policy. Normalization under high-stakes accountability draws educators further from the pedagogical relation, displacing philosophy of education and ethical practice. As a result, the creeping expansion of normalizing discipline calls into question the status of the educated self. In subsequent chapters, I use this discussion to craft an alternative relational ethic.

To address normalization in this chapter, I focus on Foucault's work about the disciplinary power of knowledge in *Discipline and Punish: The Birth of the Prison* (1995/1975). In this text, Foucault presents an historical analysis, using what he calls a genealogical method, of the changing roles that prisons and incarceration have played in Western culture. Gail McNicol Jardine (2005) defines genealogy as "Foucault's term for the investigation of the meaning of a concept through history into our own time" (p. 22), taking into account its use, purpose, and value through time. In this genealogy, Foucault shows how the institution of the prison reflects and also participates in the cultural construction of such notions as the soul and the modern self. These notions are revealed by considering the role that imprisonment is expected to play in reforming the soul and/or the self. Ultimately Foucault directs his analysis to the larger role of discipline in a myriad of institutions—including education and social science, both relevant for understanding accountability policy—and the ways in which these institutions, separately and together, participate in the discipline of the modern self.

One of the ways in which discipline occurs is through normalization, which Foucault names as the process in which a norm is named, reinforced, and refined. This norm is reified as rational, natural, and standard, with deviations from the norm named as irrational, unnatural or substandard. In education in particular, deviations from the norm can be termed exceptional, extraordinary, or gifted in some way, or sinister, dangerous, or deficient in some other way. Several significant historical aspects of normalization emerge: one is that when looking at previous periods of history, what counts as acceptable (and how things count as acceptable) shifts dramatically; another is that earlier eras are often interpreted anachronistically to support (and further normalize) contemporary notions of the normal. Foucault argues that through the genealogical method, we should uncover taken-for-granted assumptions or, as he says, our silent thinking, so as to open up the possibility for thinking differently.

To be clear, Foucault is not looking for a hidden core or some essential notion of human nature that culture obfuscates. The taken-for-granted assumptions Foucault identifies are rather fundamental cultural themes. The self, sexuality, health, and sanity are among the themes he addresses in *Discipline and Punish* and his other related work. In his work on sexuality, for example, Foucault demonstrates how a notion of what is normal sexual behavior takes form over time, while at the same time, the notion of what is sexually normal reflects, relies upon, and helps to create an underlying notion of a normal self.

Foucault is after a theorization of selfhood in light of these complex exercises of power upon the modern self. He suggests that the modern self is so caught up in the historically situated disciplinary processes that thinking differently is necessary if we are to act differently, first of all, and more so to act ethically. In the context of high-stakes accountability, the examination plays a particularly effective role in foreclosing opportunities for student self-constitution. Schools are encouraged to talk about scores rather than students, scores rather than learning or becoming. At the surface, at stake in such an arrangement, where standardized tests have taken on outsize influence, is the altering of teaching content and practices to serve instrumental goals.

More deeply, what is at stake? Foucault is on to something more radical, more fundamental to modern life. Recall that as Biesta (2004) argues, a danger when teachers become responsible for scores rather than students is that students become valued for their ability to score (and parents of kids at grade level and above are valued for their ability to choose a school). The situation reflects a twisted and upside-down power dynamic. Foucault (1995/1975) describes this power dynamic as a reversal, because what has happened is that we have substituted the student-as-subject with the student-as-measured-object. As an alternative history of testing and its importance in our current context, Foucault's historical study of disciplinary institutions provides some guidance on how we have gotten to this point and why it is so difficult to get out of it.

Many educators who read *Discipline and Punish* find it to be pessimistic and question its application to everyday educational practice. Since the book likened organized schooling (and other social institutions) to a prison, it has led many educators to reject Foucault and perhaps even other postmodern or post-structural theorists as being unconcerned with agency, politics, or a hopeful perspective on human flourishing. Like they sometimes do with other contemporary social theory, some educators dismiss *Discipline and Punish* as merely playful historicizing (or "ludic postmodernism"). Digging deeper into Foucault and the Foucault scholarship in education helps work through the pessimism and appreciate just how important normalization is to our current context and more importantly, how we might think differently about our ethical response to the disciplinary nature of schooling.

Philosophers early on worked with Foucault's ideas to explore changing relations in schools as a result of reform efforts for greater excellence in schools in the 1980s, such as those recommended in *A Nation at Risk,* the 1983 report by the National Commission on Excellence in Education that argued that national standards for education were too low and that the poor quality of education was putting the United States at economic risk. Philosophers of education have addressed many of the issues of Foucauldian normalization in education in their analyses of previous reform movements (Pignatelli, 1993), and in regard to disability (Erevelles, 2002), performativity (Kohli, 1999), environmental education (Gruenewald, 2004), research (Blacker, 1998), and sexuality (Mayo, 1998). Other work is more generally concerned with the exercise of power in education (Fendler, 2004; Ford, 2003; Franzosa, 1992; Garrison, 1998; Lechner, 2001; Masschelein, 2004; Popkewitz, 1991; Popkewitz & Brennan, 1997; Stone, 2005). Previous arguments not only named national reform discourse as normalizing but also foretold the increasing creep of normalizing practices in schools that have come in the wake of NCLB.

Susan Franzosa (1992), for example, used Foucault to talk about the role of resistance in the constitution of the self, and she tapped into trends that were just then beginning in public education. Her work anticipated what was to come:

> By normalizing a dominant ideological perspective, schooling functions to conceal and repress alternative and dissenting perspectives. As socializing

agents, schools classify, transmit, evaluate, and make coherent a partisan version of what knowledge is of most worth. They have an explicit warrant to define, codify, and teach the terms in which individuals, their world, and their interactions will have social significance. (p. 397)

Thomas Popkewitz (1991), as I discuss later in this chapter in more detail, was also well ahead of the curve, noticing and commenting on how Foucauldian discipline had a foothold on curriculum practices and reform strategies before any accountability system was in place.

Reading and reflecting on Foucault can be particularly helpful now that high-stakes testing has become the prominent method (a "technology") in the standards and accountability movements and has become especially powerful through the implementation of the NCLB legislation and resulting states' accountability programs. Federal preferences for "evidence-based" practices, "scientific" educational research, and experimental design (Feuer et al., 2002) are all relevant in Foucault's conceptualization of the "technology of the examination," and as I explain later, the power of the tests lies in how they are used and misused, more so than in how lawmakers, test authors, and psychometricians intend for them to be used. The high stakes attached to examinations enable further examination and objectification, despite the recommendations to the contrary from educational evaluators, who suggest the importance of "smart accountability" (Rogers, 2005), more responsible accountability (Sirotnik, 2004), and the growth and development of alternative forms of assessment (American Evaluation Association [AEA], 2002). Despite evaluators' cautions, the tests get used in new ways that are unintended, and with every new use, they are treated as real and meaningful.

The current importance attached to high-stakes testing and accountability, "authorized" by a common sense misunderstanding of the efficacy of educational measurements, serves a confluence of interests and desires. "Authorized" is more accurate here, rather than a blander phrase like "based on" or a stronger philosophical word like "justified." Neither of those other terms captures the political connotation of the word "authorized." In this sentence, it highlights a political state of affairs; it is *possible* for high-stakes testing to increase in importance, because enough people in enough contexts are willing to accept the authority of test scores.

In the explicitly political arena of lawmaking, high-stakes testing is a desirable tool: lawmakers can garner support for accountability legislation from those who wish for schools to be more accountable. High-stakes testing draws in multiple constituencies: advocates for high standards, taxpayers who want accountability for their tax dollars, advocates for poor children, corporate entities that may profit from newly needed tests and test preparation materials, charter school advocates, cyberschool and homeschooling advocates, and others with an interest in effecting broad change in public education. It is no wonder then that NCLB earned broad and bipartisan support when it was passed. Faith in testing further authorized high-stakes accountability, from a scientific standpoint, even though assessment experts knew at the time that accountability programs would require more tests (and more specific tests) than currently were available, and educational researchers knew there was scant research basis for the efficacy of rewards and sanctions for building the capacity of educators and schools to meet the needs of children throughout the education sector.

Critics point out the certain interests that are particularly well served by accountability policy. High-stakes accountability feeds upon neoliberal distrust of public institutions, and as I explained in the last chapter, it relies heavily upon the conflation of the exercise of democracy with consumer choice. Looking through the lens of Foucault places the phenomenon of high-stakes accountability policy into the larger context of the role that schooling plays in the constitution of the modern self.

How does power work?

Before going forward, I pull together here various hints I have dropped already in the first four chapters about how power seems to work in high-stakes accountability policy. Foucault's post-structural or postmodern articulation of power is distinct from other discussions of power and authority. For Foucault, power is not a resource that one possesses, nor is it something available to persons by virtue of their class position, gender, race, sexual preference, or ability, or any other identifiable trait, life history, or capital. Nor is power necessarily a resource built into positions of authority. It is not that all of these things are unimportant for power, because they are indeed, but for Foucault, power is something at work. One exercises power, but that does not mean that it is one's to give, to distribute, or to keep, for that would make it a resource and somehow inherent. It is continuous and continuing; one does not transcend power relations, coming to a more enlightened position that absolves oneself of having to worry about power again. There are neither privileged knowledge positions nor privileged relations. There is privilege in every position and relation. Relations are always characterized by inequalities, contingencies, and the potential for resistance. Power relations and exercises of power are unavoidable and indeed essential to our work as educators.

The relationality of power is not to suggest that power is private or entirely individualized. Indeed, larger social structures are always at play for the ways in which they influence our thinking. Regimes of truth, Foucault says, influence what we believe to be true and what we take for granted. Structures in society (and significantly for a large part of his work, structures of language) influence what we believe to be possible to know, to be, and to do. While these influences are unavoidable, it is not Foucault's project to argue for a perfect or core self that would serve as a pure alternative. Only inferentially and subliminally throughout *Discipline and Punish* does he argue against neoMarxist notions of critical consciousness, for instance. He instead builds his social theory around the insight that as selves we use structures, regimes of truth and constitute ourselves continually. As Jardine (2005) notes, it is not Foucault's project to argue against these structures but "toward understanding how one forms their own self-identity while nonetheless being affected by such systems and regimes" (p. 16).

One also exercises power over oneself, and based on what I have said already, it may be clear to the reader how that might work. One acts based upon what one believes to be true, good, beautiful, possible, or desirable. Structures and regimes of truth influence those beliefs, and so, one's actions are influenced and constrained, but not determined, by structures and regimes of truth. While it is not possible to escape power completely, there is always the potential for resistance. Significantly, it is not necessarily negative or limiting to acquiesce; and also, it is not necessarily productive to resist. Instead, for Foucault, what we can do is to understand how power works, to be vigilant for how we exercise it, and to be attentive to dangers.

Power relations are at issue in all our social institutions, such as prisons, hospitals, clubs, and schools. Conditions are in place that facilitate and constrain power relations. Schools are social institutions in which we come into constant contact with regimes of truth, structures, and power relations. The compulsory nature of public schooling, the differential ages and statuses between various persons within the school, the diverse cultures and subcultures within our population, widespread childhood poverty, and competing notions of the meaning of education make for messy, multiple, entangled power relations.

Accountability policy has made it all the more volatile. Itself a complicated series of exercises of power, accountability policy sets up conditions within which additional power relations occur. This is unavoidable and, again, essential to our work as educators. If we ignore power relations, they do not go away; we remain exercising power relations continually.

The normalized self

A pernicious aspect of the disciplinary process of normalization is how the individual becomes at the same time homogenized and reindividualized. The homogenous is the normal, and the reindividualized subject is the compendium of deviations from the normal, an obedient subject, who "acquires, through disciplinary operations, an assortment of partitioned object ranks or stations" (Pignatelli, 1993, p. 413). Foucault (1995/1975) says the following:

> In a sense, the power of normalization imposes homogeneity; but it individualizes by making it possible to measure gaps, to determine levels, to fix specialties and to render the differences useful by them one to another. It is easy to understand how the power of the norm functions within a system of formal equality, since within a homogeneity that is the rule, the norm introduces, as a useful imperative and as a result of measurement, all the shading of individual differences. (p. 184)

To normalize is not to make everyone the same, in other words. While it sounds like a paradox, the reindividualized subject loses its individuality, because it is still judged in relation to what is normal; there is no special character, but a series of deviant characteristics. As Foucault tells us, these technologies enable science effectively to remake the individual as a *case*, made up of a series of measurable characteristics.

It is the task of the examination to remake the individual. As Foucault (1995/1975) puts it:

> The examination combines the techniques of an observing hierarchy and those of a normalizing judgement. It is a normalizing gaze, a surveillance that makes it possible to qualify, to classify and to punish. It establishes over individuals a visibility through which one differentiates them and judges them. (p. 184)

It is not simply that examinations have the effect of categorizing students and making work more efficient. It more basically establishes the ability of social scientists to study students as individual cases—as examples, different from each other, positioned in relation to a standard, such as "grade level."

For Foucault (1995/1975), the ultimate role of the examination (and what has made it so troubling in high-stakes testing) is that the subject is turned into an object:

> In it are combined the ceremony of power and the form of the experiment, the deployment of force and the establishment of truth. At the heart of the procedures of discipline, it manifests the subjection of those who are perceived as objects and the objectification of those who are subjected. (p. 185)

The examination thus effects a doubled reversal of power relations—the measurement supplants the self, and measuring becomes the project of school.

Foucault (1995/1975) likens this reversal to a similar reversal of power in medicine. He likens the rise of examinations to the growth in importance of the doctor's visit in the hospital, which originally had a less significant role in the day-to-day operation of the hospital. Over several pages of his elaboration of the genealogy of the examination, Foucault links the hospital exam with the school exam:

> Gradually, the visit became more regular, more rigorous, above all more extended: it became an ever more important part of the functioning of the hospital . . . while the hospital itself, which was once little more than a poorhouse, was to become a place of training and of the correlation of knowledge; it represented a reversal therefore of the power relations and the constitution of a corpus of knowledge. . . . Similarly, the school became a sort of apparatus of uninterrupted examination that duplicated along its entire length the operation of teaching. . . . The examination enabled the teacher, while transmitting his knowledge, to transform his pupils into a whole field of knowledge. . . . [T]he age of the "examining" school marked the beginnings of a pedagogy that functions as a science. (pp. 185–7)

Seen through this lens, high-stakes testing is an extension of the power made possible by the proliferation of the technology of the examination, and it effectuates the power reversal. With the advent of high-stakes accountability, the role of the examination has never been more powerful.

Long lost, among other things, is the linkage between the measures and their history. They become tools of normalization: for categorizing students, teachers, and schools, because policy makers have deemed it necessary. The examination is a convenient technology and makes the categorization possible. The lives of students, turned into normalized objects of study, become cases of their own deviance. Through the technology of the examination, institutional practices of diagnosis, placement, and standard setting have become possible. Measured as such, students become gifted, disabled, deficient, or any other term. To paraphrase James Marshall (1996), talk of students' abilities reifies the notion that giftedness, disability, deficiency, etc., are real entities. To use Marshall's language, schools reify the measurement; they conflate the person with the measurement and what is measured.

This is in contrast to what traditional philosophy of science tells us, owing to its basis in traditional epistemology, namely that knowledge is built upon beliefs that we are justified in believing to be true. The examination becomes powerful not because of an epistemological basis, but because of the way in which it is used (by how power is exercised through its use). That is again why it makes sense to speak of the examination as being powerful because of what it authorizes, instead of, for instance, what it justifies. The examination does not justify anything in the sense of providing a foundation of truth upon which claims related to the examination are made. No psychometrician being careful about his or her epistemological foundations would make such a claim. A standardized test is a probabilistic (fallible, approximate) measurement of aptitude, achievement, or whatever else it is supposed to approximate.

In educational policy and practice, social science unwittingly contributes to normalization, because of what its tools—standardized testing, for example—make possible, necessary, or desirable. Measuring characteristics can become increasingly problematic as the use of measurements expands into the educational practices of teachers, school boards, and policy makers. As the use of such measurements makes its way into daily practice, the utility of the measured object (for example, as the starkly normalized "grade-level" student) leads to the development of new technologies, new practices, and new institutions.

The notion of "grade level" is a rather complex and powerful technology of normalization. This seductive concept has an interesting history that has been reified in new ways through high-stakes accountability policy. To act on the notion of grade level, particularly to use it to make policy or to make decisions about which students of a certain age can progress to the next grade level with their peers, relies upon a rather extensive series of decisions. What it means for a child to be at grade level depends upon essentialized notions of how children develop, how they respond to certain types of learning experiences, which learning material is appropriate at certain ages, what counts as an appropriate method to assess learning (such as but not limited to questions on a standardized test), and what counts as an acceptable range of responses to particular questions. The grade level is, in other words, a rather tangled technology of social constructions, each embedded with normalizing judgments. It is a calculation of characteristics, based upon a set of scientific practices (sometimes rigorously researched and sometimes not, but nevertheless conjectural and socially constructed), and dependent ultimately on a fixed notion of the educated self.

When new exercises of power proliferate, normalization creeps into new institutional arrangements. Testing systems contribute to creep, for instance, when they authorize judgments about such notions as student achievement, teacher quality, and school success. Other technologies seem to become thought of as necessary—such as testing regimens implemented by school districts with greater regularity and at lower grade levels than federal law requires. Measurements are of course approximations, more or less crude, depending on how carefully they have been designed, but important for Foucault's notion of power is that the power of a measurement is not in what goes into it and not what its designers intend but *in what use is made of it.*

Pignatelli (2002) describes the constraints associated with high-stakes accountability in the following passage from his essay on the ways in which surveillance constrains the practice of educational leaders:

> Regrettably, matters of curriculum, school organization and culture, and professional development as collaborative responses to the school community's collective needs and aspirations are being buried under a blanket of surveillance, shrouded in a haze of frightfully crude and narrowly defined performance indicators. (p. 171)

As Pignatelli and others have argued, there is additional concern for the ways in which high-stakes accountability compromises educators themselves as subjects, constraining their latitude for developing educational philosophies and exercising professional judgment.

For example, imagine the new power relations created when a superintendent implements new testing requirements in the second grade for the first time, ostensibly to help teachers identify children for remediation before third grade, when their test scores are incorporated into the school district's rating in the state's accountability system. This decision may lead to more structured, test-driven curriculum and instructional practices among teachers concerned that their students may face harm if they perform poorly. (Mathison and Freeman [2003] refer to a similar example.) The exercises of power in this example are multiple. Individuals—the superintendent, the teachers—make judgments in response to their conditions and create new structures and conditions that further ascribe meaning and power to testing. Individuals in effect are making decisions that call into play conflicted notions about the meaning and value of testing. They create new notions and new conditions which others respond to—teachers act then within these new conditions, perhaps adjusting their curriculum and instruction to fit the tested material, and all the while the test measurement is lent greater credence. Individuals in groups, such as school boards and policy making bodies, likewise act in ways in which they exercise power. They create institutional practices and authorize social arrangements that constrain or enable subsequent individual actions. As I mention above, the language of cause and effect is not accurate in this instance. It is not even necessary for one action to precede the other, for that matter. Individuals and individuals in groups act within the conditions in which they find themselves, or even, at times, in *anticipation* of conditions that they may foresee. The stories of Sam and Sid are replete with examples of teachers acting or proposing to act because they could anticipate what *might* happen, what their superiors *might require of them*. This is not at all surprising, since many teachers seem to be waiting always for the next shoe to drop. Those concerned about their careers and their families may be wise to get a jump on it before it happens. In Pennsylvania, we are treated to possible futures when we hear about the proposed bills before our legislature. After enough legislative seasons, some seemingly absurd proposals start to sound plausible, and educators in schools and schools of education engage in a kind of educational policy parlor game imagining how a seemingly impossible idea may become a state policy by figuring out whose interest may be served by the policy coming to fruition (lately the policies seem to be skipping that initial phase). The next phase of the game, of course, is figuring out how to respond or create something despite, but I am getting a little ahead of myself.

How did we get here?

To understand the volatile effect of accountability policy on power relations, we should hone in on high-stakes testing, the centerpiece technology of the accountability movement. Two histories, a specific history of standardized testing and a genealogy of the examination in the role of modern life, help make it clearer. First, educators need some recent educational history. As it should be noted, there has been a conflict in the educational discourse for decades. The specter of testing has haunted public education since the time of Dewey and Thorndike around the turn of the twentieth century, giving rise over time to a science of education and ongoing uneasiness about its influence on educational practice. Lagemann (2000) provides a compelling history of educational research in the twentieth century that places the debates over measurement in the larger context of the development of educational scholarship. Ambivalence about the importance of testing has roots in fundamental conflicts about the nature of knowledge (and the role of social science in producing knowledge) that existed long before Dewey or Thorndike (Crotty, 1998; Paul, 2005). The conflicts lay in tension throughout the twentieth century, but the influence of the examination is now so strong, political dominance has completely overcome scientific reason.

The use of standardized testing could be construed as innocuous enough, as long as the measurement maintains its role as a silent arbiter. As Linn (2000) points out, this can only be the case as long as schools do not actively engage in practices designed to inflate the measurement artificially. Justifications for accountability systems resound with assurances of local control and concern for children not well served by public schools. The content of the standards are the province of the states, instruction is the province of the schools themselves, accountability schemes are the silent arbiters of differences in school quality, and parents are ostensibly the ultimate arbiters of school survival. With this seemingly objective transparency (which the policy desires and relies upon for its rationalization), teachers and principals are supposed to be motivated to do what is best for children—they will do what it takes, quit, or be fired. (I imagine that only teachers and school leaders in target schools quite know the power of this little phrase.) With transparency, parents may freely choose what is best for their children, who may all finally take advantage of the promise of public education for individual emancipation.

These promises lacked precedent or basis in research when they were first proposed in pre-NCLB accountability states, and subsequently these policy promises have been shown to be contradictory. From the standpoint of a philosopher of education, the contradictions and constraints are also apparent in their founding rhetoric. For instance, North Carolina's accountability program, a rewards-and-sanctions precursor to NCLB that began in 1995, was called the ABCs of Public Education (and still is in 2011), with the A, B, and C each standing for a rhetorical pillar of the policy. "C" stood for "local control"; the idea was that schools could decide locally how to make "A" (achievement) happen, as long as the "Bs" (basics) were covered (Gunzenhauser & Gerstl-Pepin, 2002). Many educators were confused by the juxtaposition of these three concepts in the policy, since for many of them, they saw for the first time the state explicitly exerting its control over their practice. The control shift was so powerful, in fact, that it required injecting life into the previously ineffectual State Board of Education and eviscerating the formerly powerful State Department of Public Instruction. Even "Basics" caused some head scratching by educators who had been around long enough to remember the Basic Education Plan, a plan that expanded the curriculum and for a time even funded arts teachers. In the ABCs, Basics seemed to mean the tested areas of reading, math, and writing, taking the state back a step in its previous attempt to enrich the curriculum across the state.

Similarly, in its rhetoric, NCLB advocates no particular forms of curriculum or instruction, just "what works," determined "scientifically" (Feuer et al., 2002). As I argued in Chapter 1, the high-stakes testing regimen encourages a narrowed curriculum and a narrow philosophy of education, so that it becomes difficult to even dialogue about alternative philosophies of education and the default philosophy of education becomes easier. Similarly, the details about what counted as "what works" and what was named as "scientific research" merely supported the default philosophy of education, because of a Congressional narrowing of an already narrow National Research Council definition of what should count as scientific educational research (Eisenhart & DeHaan, 2005; St. Pierre, 2002). An educator no less mainstream than Arne Duncan has come out in opposition to the ways in which NCLB has contradicted its rhetoric and constricted its curriculum, as he indicates in an interview transcript:

> I also worry a lot about the narrowing of the curriculum under No Child Left Behind. Too many schools are focusing on just what's tested so there's a loss of PE [physical education], music, art, the nontested subjects, even science in some places. . . . So how are we going to think differently about

that? How are we going to make sure that we're giving all children a well-rounded education from the earliest ages on? (Richardson, 2009, pp. 25–6)

In the same interview, Duncan advocates national standards and national testing, however, so similarly to Finn (2010), he does not see high-stakes accountability policy as fundamentally at odds with the interests he expresses about nontested areas. While not as stridently as Finn, Duncan seems to hold schools responsible for constricting the curriculum.

As a further point, it should be clear by now that power works with such great complexity in institutions such as public schools that someone in Duncan's position should not make such statements without appreciating some irony. As the research on the effects of high-stakes accountability suggests, even these local conversations, when they are encouraged, are constrained by the discourses that participants bring to the dialogue. The dialogues that standards and accountability engender, as some theorists have shown, may be unrecognizable as dialogue. Popkewitz (1991), as I mentioned before an early theorist to apply Foucault to educational policy, has noted the ways in which educational policy co-opts dialogue through disciplinary practices intended to reduce its effects. Popkewitz names the "rhetoric of participation," in which schools are seen to be democratic because of "input" from "representatives" during processes of goal setting or curriculum development. Teachers supposedly participate in the development of state standards, for example, but that participation does not necessarily resemble a democratic process. Often policy restrains the dialogue, or the forms of assessment limit possibilities. When the goals are constrained, Popkewitz refers to that situation as an example of *instrumental rationality* (as opposed to a similar situation which would evidence *substantive rationality*, in which the goals of the task or project would be open ended):

> Participation formed within an instrumental rationality contains two seemingly different implications for social regulation. The administrative rules distance participants from the sources of interest involved through the distinctions and categories formed. Attention is not directed to specific people who form the rules, but to the regulations that focus attention on what the program requires. No person or agency seems in control. Responsibility for the quality of teaching and teacher education becomes diffused through the symbolic rituals of democracy, while various patterns of social regulation proliferate ostensibly to ensure accountability. (p. 214)

In this passage, Popkewitz articulates the ways in which disciplinary practices simultaneously encourage dialogue and neutralize it. In the name of standardization, dialogue becomes a ritual of diffusion. Instrumental rationality reigns, guiding participants to meet disembodied goals; participation further diffuses responsibility. Decision making becomes anonymous and distanced from actual practices and the meanings of those practices.

Teaching practices respond to these decisions rather than participate in them; teachers respond by following the already constrained curriculum and adapting their practices to it, and they have no reason to expect their participation in the dialogue about goals. It is easy to understand within this type of system why prepackaged, "teacher proof" practices would be desirable. If the tag signifying that these practices have been "scientifically proven effective" can be attached to it, canned curriculum and instruction is possible, desirable, and (in a regime of truth built upon the necessity for research-based practices) difficult to argue against. Educational researchers describe these rationales as "scientistic" or "scientized" (Nicholson-Goodman & Garman, 2007).

In the prescient 1991 text in which the above quotation appears, Popkewitz states what becomes possible next, what is authorized, in such practices: "New rules that routinize teachers' work have become plausible, since status is to be gained through performance tied to a notion of 'science'" (p. 216). As I have been noting all along, the choice of conceptual language is crucial here; routinized work becomes a desirable method in a school, because it keeps teachers focused on performance. To reiterate what I mentioned above about the workings of power as explained by Foucault, one does not cause the other; accountability provisions do not cause routinized practices. Instead, the conditions of accountability policy make routinized work, like canned curriculum and instruction, an understandable choice for a practice. In the conditions educators find themselves, they may enact new practices for specific reasons—for example, for job security, for status, for monetary reward, or to avoid the low-performing label. Educators' new practices in turn help establish conditions for new enactments of practices.

Control through surveillance

As others have argued, educational policy in many Western contexts, including Australia, the United Kingdom, and the United States, has undergone an increasing degree of centralized surveillance and control (Biesta, 2004; Pignatelli, 2002). High-stakes accountability systems bring the tools of social science to bear in rather explicit means of control. To reiterate, in his explanation of the normalizing functions of institutions, Foucault (1995/1975) describes the role that social science has played in creating modern individuals, providing tools for institutions that support our cultural notions of what it means to be an autonomous, educated person. Most effectively, persons discipline themselves, acting in ways that constitute themselves as docile bodies and normalized selves. The disciplined self, part and parcel of the modern "soul," Foucault argues, incorporates self-surveillance into its life (a particular kind of exercise of power over oneself). This disciplined self is problematic to the extent that discipline cuts off possibilities and choices, or more accurately the ability of the individual to see choices that have been foreclosed. As Pignatelli (1993) states, the "omnipresent threat to freedom, self-normalizing practice . . . [is] our willingness to accept and internalize questionable limits on what we can know about ourselves" (p. 412) or perhaps become.

In his classic example of self-discipline, Foucault relates the example of Jeremy Bentham's panopticon, a proposed prison structure from 1834, in which Bentham, incidentally a utilitarian philosopher more radical than Mill, arranged cells around a central surveillance point. Each inmate is invisible to any other inmate but simultaneously viewable by a single guard from the surveillance point. The inmate cannot see the guard, and so Bentham supposes that because the inmate believes that at any moment, he or she *could* be in view, the inmate disciplines himself or herself. While Bentham's prison design itself was not built, it influenced subsequent prison architecture. It is indicative of Bentham's early modern assumptions of efficient discipline, and Foucault makes the panopticon emblematic of modern disciplinary power.

Modern discipline provides a contrast to more violent medieval discipline, detailed at length in *Discipline and Punish* for its role in purifying the errant soul through torture (i.e., to exorcise its demons) and through the public spectacle of torture and execution simultaneously frightening people into obedience and reassuring them that their ruler is in control. The differing roles of discipline and punishment across historical eras reflect different purposes and meanings attributed to the disciplined self. Feudalism worked well through obedience and fealty, largely played out in public. Modern life works better if the self is self-disciplined publicly and privately.

Marshall (1996) summarizes Foucault's insight: "spaces in the new disciplinary blocks operate differently as individuals are constituted in various ways through technologies of domination and in spaces, again private, where individuals constitute themselves through technologies of the self" (p. 18). Schools do their part. In spaces such as the school, science provides efficient technologies that help this process along, including institutional practices and social arrangements that encourage discipline.

To put it all together: through the scientifically based technology of the examination, accountability policy leads to new institutional practices and social arrangements that in turn enable exercises of power wherein individuals eventually discipline themselves in private spaces. Interests of normalization find favored status as the individual is reconstituted as a case, with a set of attributes that deviate from the normal. The historical, contingent nature of the examination is forgotten, unknown (e.g., by some policy makers and others who find use for standardization), or sequestered (e.g., by testing companies and some measurement specialists, who can only hope to control the misuse of the examination by policy makers [AEA, 2002]). Foucault (1995/1975) expresses this process in more abstract terms:

> as power becomes more anonymous and more functional, those on whom it is exercised tend to be more strongly individualized; it is exercised by surveillance rather than ceremonies, by observation rather than commemorative accounts, by comparative measures that have the "norm" as reference rather than genealogies giving ancestors as points of reference; by "gaps" rather than by deeds. (p. 193)

As Foucault articulates, the examination is one of the most powerful tools of normalization. For Foucault, it is an example of what happens when "disciplinary power [becomes] an 'integrated' system, linked from the inside to the economy and to the aims of the mechanisms of power that it brought with it" (p. 176). While this may sound like a critique of current educational policy, as Foucault explains, the history of the school is a history of the exercise of power over children. The democratic aims of Horace Mann and Thomas Jefferson aside, public schooling developed partly as a way to discipline wayward youth, to get them off the streets and make them less dangerous and more useful. Over time, public schooling has continued in its role of creating and reinforcing the bounds of what it means to be normal and sorting students according to their deviation from the normal.

Evaluators remind us that test scores should only be used as one measure of student achievement, and that accountability systems can and should be designed with more precision, for instance, using multiple year measurements in place of year-to-year tests (Linn & Haug, 2002), aspects of state accountability systems that NCLB obviates (Linn, 2005). As I mentioned earlier, the misuse and misappropriation of standardized testing has made evaluation and assessment specialists critical of where accountability legislation has taken educational practice. In an official statement shortly after NCLB was approved, the American Evaluation Association (2002) urges policy makers and educators to make use of alternative and expanded forms of assessment that are readily available, rather than relying too heavily on standardized assessments.

Using testing more appropriately and developing more accurate accountability systems are logical (and instrumentally rational) goals, and such actions are laudable and necessary. At the same time, such goals underestimate the powerful effects of testing—the reversal of power that Foucault identifies. In this sense, high-stakes tests appear to be something entirely different in the context of US public education than the very same tests without high stakes being assigned to them. Psychometricians' calls for restraint are essential but perhaps ultimately fruitless given the power policy makers (and others) perceive their measurements to have to determine how well a teacher teaches, how well students learn, and the quality of a school.

Using Foucault leads to a more fundamental critique. Foucault would have us see the effects of accountability policy not solely as the misapplication of tools designed for other purposes. Foucault also helps us to see that the exercises of disciplinary power seen as a result of high-stakes accountability policy reflect something rather important and fundamental to the educational enterprise. As Foucault shows in *Discipline and Punish* (1995/1975), the institution of schooling constitutes a cultural notion of what it means to be a modern self: a disciplined, normalized, and docile subject.

The rise of the science of education has made it possible for legislators (and subsequently the public) to believe that the level of surveillance in high-stakes accountability policy is possible, plausible, and desirable. The psychometric dream has become a Foucauldian nightmare. The examination of course has a long history in education, and the district curriculum, state standards, and national standards are likewise instruments of discipline. Seen this way, high-stakes accountability policy is both a more transparent technology of control and the perfection of disciplinary surveillance.

Are educators just agents of normalization? Toward resistance

When one understands normalization and the power of the examination, it may begin to appear everywhere, and it can appear that individuals are powerless to do anything about it. Perhaps teachers working in the large, complicated social institution of the public school are just agents of control, exercising whatever power they believe they may have only to serve the interests of the larger structure or regime of truth. One can imagine the individual having very little effect. Because of this depiction, many theorists in education are ambivalent about the usefulness of Foucault for his seemingly nihilistic view of power, while others suggest that rejection comes from a fundamental misreading of Foucault and a misapprehension of the possibilities provided by viewing power as Foucauldian (Marshall, 1996; Mayo, 2000; McDonough, 1994). Others are concerned that Foucault does not adequately address collective action and therefore is limiting for work toward social justice. Foucault, especially in his later work, is very concerned that we *not* see the individual apart from the social.

We need to think through what it means to act within schools under the pressure of normalizing judgment. Following Foucault, when we grant test scores outsized power, we are exercising power over ourselves and others through individual actions, justifying our actions as necessary, beneficial, or perhaps scientific, or the dangerous catch-all, "research-based." What is necessary, beneficial, and scientific are tied up in our assumptions about the efficacy of technologies (tests and norms, for example) and the science that has gone into them. Following Foucault some more, when we exercise power, we are choosing one possibility over many others, and we fail to the extent we do not consider the possibilities that are obfuscated or foreclosed by the normalizing tendencies associated with these technologies.

As such, the effects of high-stakes accountability policy are more relevant for the individual exercises of power that educators enact and the educational experiences that result than the intentions of policy makers or the stated rationales within policies themselves. The greater impact, and the greater opportunity for dangerous results, resides in educators themselves, who enact whatever policy is established through new practices and power arrangements that children encounter on a day-to-day basis.

If we only focus on the repressive aspects of power, Foucault contends, we lack a robust formulation of the self, its constitution, and the crucial role of resistance in the constitution of the self. Further, we underestimate our complicity with normalization. For Foucault, resistance to normalization is a fundamental practice of human freedom. And because normalization for Foucault is so effectively achieved through self-discipline, Foucauldian resistance is not limited to what may immediately come to mind: questioning authority, protesting, or refusing to participate. Nor should we expect that the resistance that is called for would be necessarily limited to resistance to standards, testing, or accountability itself. It might be the opportunity to resist the deficit discourses, for instance, which certainly could be linked to standardization, but I could imagine engaging standards and culturally relevant pedagogy simultaneously as a way to resist normalization (see Skrla & Scheurich, 2004).

We should think of resistance to normalization as a more radically personal, relational stance toward oneself and others. In any individual interaction, there are power relations and the potential both for domination and resistance, because as Hoy (2004) argues, any exercise of power necessitates the possibility of resistance, for by definition it is resistance that is overcome in any exercise of power. This relation may be clearer in an example.

I now return to a previous example about a hypothetical superintendent instituting second-grade testing. In order for the examination to effect its stunning reversal of power relations, various individuals and groups have to make decisions that subjugate their own resistance. I detailed earlier examples of some of those decisions; these interactions are multiple, and they extend to everyday interactions that educators have with each other, their students, and their communities. The normalizing power of a test score or a grade level is extended any time it is reified in an interaction—when a teacher discusses a child's test score with a parent, for instance, particularly if the teacher leaves unnamed and unquestioned the historical and social construction that is the test score. We might refer to this as forgetting that the score is as unreal as it is real. Reminding ourselves and others of the contingent, constructed nature of these interactions should remind us to ask ourselves what aspects of that score's unreality we are forgetting, and how is that amnesia keeping us from treating the student as a person of possibility and not a Foucauldian case. We need to remind ourselves that when we do not remember the unreality, we are missing an opportunity for resistance. Without the possibility of resistance in each of those individual instances, in fact, it makes no sense to make the claim for exercises of power (Hoy, 2004).

But how embedded are we within social structures? How deeply are our assumptions influenced by regimes of truth? From my research, I would conclude that those assumptions are strongest and most powerful in schools so under the gun that they seem to be without the luxury or capacity to think otherwise. Target schools, those under the threat for takeover, reconstitution, or being added to the list of low-performing schools, seem to act in ways that suggest they accept the efficacy of the technologies of tests and norms; they adopt scripted curricula, they are more likely to teach to the test, and they are more likely to constrict their curricula. Schools which do not have those concerns are in a better position to have, air, and enact varied opinions about the tests and standards. In the Olympus School District, for example, Pennsylvania state standards are considered far too basic, and the broad curriculum coverage that the state tests require of schools is not much of a concern. The district has not had to worry that content is left uncovered or that its curriculum is misaligned with the state standards (Cozzolino & Bichsel, 2010).

Evidence suggests that the distinction between target and better-positioned schools is not as simple as I have just suggested, however. Recall from the RAND study (Hamilton et al., 2007) that teachers and administrators in well-positioned schools tend to believe in larger numbers that assessments are accurate measures of student learning, while those who are more likely to be subject to sanctions are much less likely to believe that. It appears that in some cases, school personnel are acting despite their beliefs. We have then a system in which the actors do not believe and which they do not trust, and moreover, they know that what they are doing is not right. This is a difficult system for anyone to sustain.

To get back to Sam and his school, in this chapter I sketched out the background to explain the workings of power in high-stakes accountability policy, as it is experienced in schools on a day-to-day basis. Sam is no doubt well-positioned at his current school and in his school district to do well in the accountability system, and he has a handle on many of the workings of power that are within his grasp to keep the normalizing pressures of the state accountability system and the national accountability policy at bay. However, we also get a sense, even from his brief story, that there are important conditions in place that could easily change his situation. Eventually the district will hire a new superintendent, and while Sam's current superintendent exerts no discernable pressure on Sam to initiate practices to inflate test scores, a new superintendent (or an unexpected new mix on the school board after the next election) could bring a new agenda that makes it more difficult for Sam to hold the line against normalization. I suspect that Sam is experienced and committed enough to handle what comes. In situations like Sam's, I am actually more concerned with succession and what a leader less skilled and with less of a memory of teaching before test-based accountability would do with the same set of conditions. I am concerned that the pressures facing new principals, even in well-positioned schools like Sam's and especially as proficiency requirements rise toward 2014, will lead young leaders to enact accountability practices and encourage normalizing practices presented to them as research-based, aligned, or any number of terms that make it easier to meet their accountability targets and keep their schools in compliance. I want new school leaders (and new teachers, for that matter) to be better prepared to enact and cultivate their professionalism.

What makes a strong, professional educator in such an accountability system? When teachers, schools, and students are all normalized by high-stakes accountability systems, where are the possibilities for action? What are the bounds for action for an educator who is both normalized and normalizing? Before I can provide a satisfactory answer to these questions, I need to explore in more detail what it may mean to act ethically as a self that is continually constituted, the project of the next chapter.

6

Care of the educated self in crisis

Iris in the middle

Iris Lorenzo is a resource teacher for middle-school children who have special needs at an urban magnet school in Western Pennsylvania. Almost two-thirds of the students in her school are African American children, and about half of the student population qualifies for free or reduced-price lunch. On most test measures, the percentage of children at her school who test as proficient is on par with the rest of the state. With significant subgroups in her school, she had been through several years of stressful pressure when she was interviewed in January 2008. While many of her colleagues in special education find the pressure upsetting, Iris describes herself as less stressed by the situation than some of her colleagues.

As part of her philosophy of education, Iris wants schools to reach all the students but without the expectation that they would all come out the same. She responds to a question about responsibility with this self-appraisal:

> In all of my classes I have levels from kids who are maybe one level below grade level and have other kids that are about five [levels below grade level]. So I have to find a way to—if I'm teaching simplifying fractions, I have to try to—accommodate the kids that have a slight learning disability with the kids that have a more significant learning disability. So I actually, instead of feeling like I'm responsible for a class as a whole, I feel like I'm responsible [for] each individual kid to try to get a concept across.

Consistent with her individual approach, Iris maintains open communication with parents and makes sure to call parents when students make important accomplishments, so that her calls are not always about problems. She works toward building mutual respect with her students. She wants them to know that she cares for them but also that she will be firm with them.

Iris' main struggle at the time of the interview was completing enough material with the students by the time that testing takes place. At any given time, she knows where she is in relation to the pace prescribed by the district. It seems to her that too much material is required by the time testing happens. She had an innovative idea to have students work in the computer lab as sports reporters: "They were sports statisticians. They loved it. They learned it better than any other class, but we can't do that. I got in trouble. Well, not in trouble." Iris then implied that no one said anything to her, but she experienced some regret about the activity when she realized how far behind that made her students when the two-week activity was over.

The special education students in her school are the one subgroup in the school that has not met AYP. She and the rest of the special education faculty feel pressure from their supervisors, but Iris has noticed that the pressure is indirect, with imprecise threats that she or the special education department may receive some sort of sanction:

> In my position we have been threatened that the Special Ed department had been told that—it's all roundabout stuff, but apparently the state had threatened that if we don't pass the AYP. . . . If that happens more than several times they could come in and start teaching us how to teach. And that's just, that's a threat. . . . It was just in our Special Ed. meeting, and nobody knew. I mean, I guess the state does have that power. . . . Our PSSA scores were actually pretty good, so nothing has happened. I remember that meeting, and there were teachers who were just almost in tears thinking that they could lose their jobs. They almost use it as a threat on you.

From her story of this situation, Iris comes across as being in opposition to unnamed supervisors. When she talks about her work with students and parents in terms that suggest she is confident about her work and her approach with parents and students, the pressure seems to place her at risk. The vaguely threatened sanctions seem impersonal:

> That's the thing. You don't know where it comes from. You don't know true or anything like that. It just has everyone in such an uproar to do well. You can already tell the tension in my building is already rising. And the writing test is in two weeks. You can already tell. The writing booklets are out.

Also of interest is that one problem the teachers encounter is that students do not seem to take the tests as seriously as the teachers do:

Maybe a couple of them do. So that's another thing we have to do is build them up. Tell them how important [the tests] are. . . . My kids don't seem so bothered but others do.

Interviewer: *How do you tell them they're important? It's important for why?*

I tell them it's important for me. . . . I told them the truth: "[if] you do bad and if you just blow it off"—[stops her thought and restarts]—I said, "If you try your hardest, I don't care if you miss every problem. But if you don't try your hardest and you sit and make flowers out of the bubbles, then I could lose my job. And then what are you going to do if some substitute comes in?" Because they hate change. Any tactic that works. Anything.

As a teacher in a school that is somewhat a target of high-stakes accountability, but which has so far met most of its accountability targets, Iris is positioned in the middle. Neither well-positioned to do well, nor an explicit low-performing target school, Iris' school needs to attend to the progress of its subgroups, which puts Iris in the middle of a pressured situation. As someone accountable for a subgroup, the whole school counts on her, and she has the presence of mind to frame her work with her students as a one-to-one responsibility she has with each student, whose progress in relation to their grade level is widely varied.

At the same time, Iris is in the middle in another important sense: between her supervisors and her students in the system of pressure for producing test score results. Her supervisors enact the anonymous power of state-level sanctions on her, vague, imprecise, yet thinly veiled threats that she needs to perform. Placed in an oppositional stance, she repeats those threats to her students, softening the threat a bit through professing to support whatever best effort the students can muster, but the threat is clear: hinging on her students' perceived dislike of change (or is it fear?), she wants them to see the (vague) threat of her dismissal as a corresponding threat to them personally.

As one reads this, the rationale for why the special education supervisors would use threats is unclear (as opposed to assessing and intentionally constructing the capacity of the special education teachers), but a potential rationale is embedded in how Iris talks about the students. They do not seem to care about the tests, she and her colleagues agree, so they need to be motivated to care. Does Iris see herself in the same position in relation to her supervisors? Do they believe she needs to be made to care about test scores? Or are they incapable of another strategy? Without good qualitative data on these questions, they remain open. At no point in the interview transcript do I get the impression that she was part of a team that had a strategy for increasing proficiency among their students. The absent presence of the school's distinct magnet philosophy in her responses to the interview questions is curious as well. Is the philosophy of education that guides the magnet considered relevant to this subgroup's test scores, and if not, which do they consider more important? In light of these unanswered questions, the individualized approach she spoke of in relation to her students might seem contradictory, or it could be the reason why she seems to be less affected than some of her colleagues.

Care of the self

As an educator in the middle, Iris experiences acquiescence and resistance simultaneously in her relations above and below her in the hierarchy of accountability policy. Iris hints at compelling exercises of power operating in her professional life, and I am most interested in the extent to which her individualized responsibility toward students is strong enough to sustain her as a professional and to sustain her students as they face the school's normalizing judgment.

In the previous chapters, I have so far presented a critique of the current context of public education under high-stakes accountability policy, and at this point, my turn is toward the active/ethical framework that I argue is needed to respond to the relational situations in which educators find ourselves. If, as I have argued, high-stakes accountability systems are technologies of normalization in which tests effect a reversal of power relations and take on outsized proportions in educational practice, what alternatives do we have? One part of building an alternative framework is countering the dominance of a nonreflective philosophy of education, which exists largely by default.

As I argued in Chapter 1, high stakes accountability policy presents a crisis of the educated self, because it authorizes practices and conditions that constrain opportunities for educators and students to constitute themselves. Unless educators attend to the implications of normalization for the constitution of the educated self, they are unlikely to curtail the largely negative effects of the high stakes (Gunzenhauser, 2006; Sirotnik, 2004). As I argued in the last chapter, the most significant actions in accountability systems are the actions that individuals make in response to those systems, whether in direct response to what they have been ordered to do, or what they do to themselves and others in response to what they are given or told to do.

I propose that by turning to a notion of the self based on work by Foucault's later work, wherein the self is continually constituted through exercises of power, we may see more clearly the extent of the crisis of the educated self that we face in education and formulate resistance to the normalizing tendencies of high-stakes accountability policy. Foucault devoted much time to his notion of the "care of the self," built upon historical critique of the modern self and the exploration of hidden possibilities through cultivation of a nonfoundational ethics.

By linking disciplinary power and the care of the self, I wish to characterize a promising form of resistance for our current educational context. As I said in Chapter 1, I argue that resistance to normalization in our current context requires caring for oneself and providing the conditions and experiences for students to care for themselves. Three projects contribute to that goal. First is developing clarity on what we mean by the educated self, a project of the philosophy of education, which I take up in this chapter. Next is fostering the ethical and professional judgment of educators, which comes in the next chapter. These projects require a complex notion of ethics and the workings of power, particularly how one thinks of oneself acting in relation to others. This third project I begin in the next chapter and wrap up in the last chapter.

What is a self for Foucault?

Within the work of Foucault, what alternatives are available to the normalization of the self which we may marshal for resistance? For a compelling answer to that question, we have to go outside *Discipline and Punish* to Foucault's later work. Complicating this effort, as Mayo (2000) points out, is the tendency when seeing things from a Foucauldian perspective to become fatalistic about the potential for resistance. As Mayo says, "readings of Foucault that make power inescapable appear to foreclose the possibility of action" (p. 116). However, here is where Foucault can be most helpful:

> While work on Foucault's implications for education helps to overcome naïve hopes about the emancipatory potential of education, he has not been sufficiently harnessed to the project of negotiating the difficult pull between domination and resistance, the process of normalization and formation of hypercritical communities. (Mayo, 2000, p. 103)

Beyond cultivating cynicism or hypercritical communities, what does Foucault leave us with for addressing the normalization of the self? If high-stakes accountability is characterized as a project of normalization of the self, what notions of the self should educators consider instead? What might these notions of "other selves" be—selves not quite so normalized (if that is possible)? Without radical attention to what we mean by the self, whatever successor reforms are imagined and whatever forms of resistance are assembled, public education is likely to continue to expand its project of the normalization of the subject and do it through us educators. This project was well in place before the advent of high-stakes accountability policy, and we now take it for granted.

Articulating a Foucauldian self is an extensive, lengthy, and contested task. Despite the difficulty of nailing down a Foucauldian self, the utility of a Foucauldian notion of the self, as I hope to show, is that it may form the basis for educators to engage productively with various others about differing notions of the educated self, differing notions of educational aims, and differing philosophies of education. Several theorists have specifically used the Foucauldian self to talk about resistance to the demands of high-stakes accountability (Pignatelli, 2002; Zembylas, 2003).

In search of a Foucauldian self

I present a synthesis of the scholarship on the Foucauldian self to orient the reader toward the more extended explication to come. In sum, the self can be characterized by four initial features. First, a self is not a core identity or essence but instead a continual process of self-constitution. Second, the self is constituted constantly and unavoidably through power relations with others and through exercises of power over oneself. Third, as a constituting self, this self is not another version of the humanist self as existing in nature as essentially and primordially free, but instead this self may instead be said to participate in a process of freeing through pursuing possibilities. Fourth, this self is opened to possibility through disruptive differences. These are introduced in turn and then explained in greater detail below.

Self-constitution

Primarily, following Foucault, there is not an authentic, other self that stands in opposition to the normalized self. The subject is neither an essence to be discovered nor a core to be uncovered. The project of the self, Foucault contends, is its constant constitution. As Pignatelli (1993) explains, "Foucault takes as the project of modernity the continual project of self-invention, not self-discovery; the challenge of surprising oneself, the testing and reassessing of who one really is in the presence of an active and productive imagining" (p. 418). As Michalinos Zembylas (2003) puts it, "the self is continuously constituted, never completed, never fully coherent, never completely centered securely in experience. Foucault does not refer to any primordial experience but to the relations between forms of subjectivity and kinds of normalizing practices" (p. 113). This notion of how the self is constituted suggests an emphasis away from predetermined outcomes of educational experiences, and not even outcomes so much as the experiences themselves.

Self and power

Foucault's notion of power as a relation (as opposed to a resource or a commodity), ever present in action and unreliably positive or negative, has implications for the self as well. As both an agent of power and a subject of exercises of power, often at the same time, the self is constituted through power relations. The project of the self is not simply the unshackling of repressive forces. If emancipation is the goal, we would have to redefine emancipation as a continual process, or perhaps even an orientation toward freedom. Further, one's actions may as easily oppress as they liberate. It is incumbent upon one to be aware of one's positioning in relation to others and in relation to structural arrangements and regimes of truth.

The educator who attempts to exercise power does not act from a position of privileged authority or privileged knowledge (Vinson & Ross, 2003). When he speaks of teachers' power, Pignatelli (1993) warns against "grand configurations of what it means for teachers to be 'empowered' or to exercise their agency" (pp. 411–12). He instead wants them to be mindful that "reform efforts [are] important opportunities to develop and to frame ongoing critical strategies that not only challenge prevailing inequitable structural arrangements, but also probe their own complicity in those arrangements" (p. 412). The self is in a sense a dangerous actor, the teacher not a hero but one exercising power, and in Pignatelli's formulation, aware not only of one's limits but also of oneself as implicated in oppressive relations.

Self and possibility

The self, not empowered so much as continually constituting itself through power relations, may still work toward freedom, if as Pignatelli (1993) and others suggest, we understand that freedom, like the self, is not a state of human nature. Freedom is instead for Foucault a practice of "opening up to different possibilities, to ways of seeing ourselves and our practices differently by attempting to identify the arbitrary in what may appear to be fundamental or essential" (Pignatelli, 1993, pp. 417–18). The practice of freedom in other words is a stance in relation to certainty, doubt about the surety of foundations and essences, a radical appreciation for "persistent critique" (St. Pierre, 2002), not for the sake of critique but for the possibilities that may arise.

Self and difference

Foucauldian and other alternative notions of the self emphasize the significance of difference. The self that is open to possibility is nurtured by attending to difference. The self is challenged to see possibility by heeding different voices (Biesta, 1998), by fostering abilities to listen to difference (Garrison, 1996), by inquiring into the particular (Pignatelli, 1993), and by engaging in experiences that disrupt one's assumptions (Infinito, 2003). Interaction with other selves who are different is a significant aspect of the philosophies of education of Greene (1988) and Dewey (1966/1916, 1997/1938). Echoing Foucault and his notion of power, Greene has this to say about the significance of difference (in this case, plurality):

> When we think of the diverse and pluralist society we have been describing, we need then to have in mind a range of individuals or groups confronting a field of possibilities in which varied ways of behaving and reacting may be realized. (p. 116)

The Foucauldian self, in greater detail

In this section, I go into greater detail about the idea of the Foucauldian constituting self. Theorists have turned to the later work of Foucault to articulate a notion of a constituting self. The first place that many readers have consulted is Foucault's three-volume history of sexuality—*The History of Sexuality* (1990/1976), *The Use of Pleasure* (1985/1984), and *The Care of the Self* (1986/1984)—wherein Foucault looks to Ancient Greece for a hermeneutics of desire and finds a hermeneutics of the subject. It amounts to an extension on his discussion of the modern self and the beginning of his formulation of a subsequent ethics.

A nonauthentic self

Foucault characterizes his evolving project in the three volumes of the history of sexuality as an articulation of the ways in which Greeks thought of man (sic) as a subject. He says the following in the second volume about his project as a historical and philosophical analysis:

> a history of the way in which individuals are urged to constitute themselves as subjects of moral conduct would be concerned with the models proposed for setting up and developing relationships with the self, for self-reflection, self-knowledge, self-examination, for the decipherment of the self by oneself, for the transformations that one seeks to accomplish with oneself as object. (Foucault, 1985/1984, p. 29)

Already with this quotation, one gets a sense that by talking about "a relationship with the self" and the "transformations one seeks to accomplish with oneself," Foucault departs from a notion of the self as the core of one's identity, something to uncover over time, an essence to discover, or a pure, foundational notion of human nature (Marshall, 1996). The self appears instead to be a project.

Much of Foucault's discussion of sexuality aims to reinterpret Ancient Greek notions of the self, which Foucault argues have been distorted by anachronistic interpretation and appropriation by modern thinkers. Foucault (1984/1985) reminds his reader that, while there was great diversity of thought in Ancient Greece, much of the arguments about how the self goes about its business had to do with understanding one's passions and mastering them:

> The accent was placed on the relationship with the self that enabled a person to keep from being carried away by the appetites and pleasures, to maintain a mastery and superiority over them, to keep his senses in a state of tranquility, to remain free from interior bondage to the passions, and to achieve a mode of being that could be defined by the full enjoyment of oneself, or the perfect supremacy of oneself over oneself. (p. 31)

This self engages in a process of seeking tranquility. The language in this quotation suggests aspects of the Foucauldian self that he explores elsewhere—namely the sense in which the self works on its own transformation. The Foucauldian self is a work in progress, neither the search for one's core identity nor the discovery of the truth about oneself.

By turning to this more contingent theory of the self, Foucault's approach is to object to an "*a priori* theory of the subject, that is, any theory about the subject that does not take the theorizing activity of that subject itself into account" (Biesta, 1998, p. 7), which he attributes to the "Cartesian moment" (Foucault, 2005/2001), when the mind and body are split and the rational mind is the leader of the body. In this sense, Foucault articulates a postmodern alternative, drawing from traditions of thought but not tying himself to a unitary notion of a self, whether that self is characterized as being in equilibrium, reaching self-actualization, or achieving rationality—all concepts upon which modern ethics are based. Such bases or definitions of the self would underestimate the effect of power: the way in which structures and regimes of truth come into play through our relations with others and the ways in which we discipline ourselves.

As Biesta (1998) explains, "postmodernism implies a crisis of the subject, it is a crisis of modern man . . ., [the] eventual erasure of the modern *articulation* of subjectivity" (p. 7). Subjectivity remains but is redefined, in other words. Rather than being a project of vigilance over our authenticity, selves can work on their subjectivity through vigilance against domination and the lack of choice (Infinito, 2003). Turning to a notion of a postmodern self can then be freeing in an important way. On this issue, Lynda Stone (2005) intones: "Giving up a modern 'search for certainty,' to use Dewey's idiom, need not be cause for despair. It can, instead, be 'liberating,' a freeing up to be, to live, to act" (p. 39).

Self-constitution

Foucault shifts our attention to the *constitution* of the self, a nonfoundational formulation. It is, as Marshall (2001) suggests, an emphasis on a theory of "*how* we constitute the self" (p. 83). As Zembylas (2003) explains, "In Foucault's writings, the unified self is challenged and fragmented; he uses the term 'subjectivity' instead of 'selfhood' or 'self-identity' to describe the manifold ways in which individuals are historically constituted" (p. 113). "Fragmented" is apt. In contrast to some of the interpretations of Foucault as nihilistic, giving up the unity of the subject fragments subjectivity but does not erase the subject itself (Biesta, 1998). Some modern notions are lost here, but I mean "lost" in the sense of lost baggage, previous necessities that we discover we can flourish better without hanging onto them.

Significant for Foucault is turning away from the necessity of purifying the self, for eliminating elements of deficiency that cloud the true identity of the self, which Justen Infinito (2003) describes as another form of normalization, "the insistence that individuals be constantly vigilant about uncovering the 'truth' about themselves" (p. 72). The distinction between being authentic and constituting oneself emerges most clearly in *The Hermeneutics of the Subject* (2001/2005), a series of lectures wherein Foucault uses genealogical analysis to address the Ancient Greek exhortation to "know thyself," which Foucault depicts as fundamental to modern notions of the self as needing to be authentic or true to one's nature or to a coherent notion of human nature. Foucault contextualizes the exhortation to "know thyself," suggesting instead that Greeks had a different, more humble idea in mind:

> As for the [exhortation to] "know yourself," this was the principle [that] you should always remember that you are only a mortal after all, not a god, and that you should neither presume too much on your strength nor oppose the powers of the deity. (p. 4)

Foucault uses this insight to think differently about the care of the self, a concept he contends had greater relevance to the Greeks than the less significant (and later misunderstood) exhortation to "know thyself." This notion of the care of the self provides him ways for reimagining ethics and selfhood.

The never-completed, never-coherent self Foucault names leads to significantly altered projects of the self. Although power is always operating,

Foucault does not see power as determining our actions, because the self is itself a form of power (Infinito, 2003). The self can develop and transform (Marshall, 2001), and it can "transgress the given, to create ourselves as something 'other'" (Infinito, 2003, p. 71). As Marshall says, "power is productive, it creates or makes people" (p. 84). This distinction in Foucault's formulation of power places creation in opposition to constraint. The subject is a form of power, and self-creation is itself an exercise of power:

> The "subject" is not some entity with defined characteristics, according to Foucault; the subject *is* a form of power at the same time that it is the product of power. It would seem that the *free* subject is a form of power that is aware of itself as a power. . . . The method of "coming to be" such a subject will also be an active process, an exercise of power. (Infinito, 2003, p. 72)

As Infinito argues, the constitution of the self through an active process of exercises of power is precisely the source of an ethics and resistance. In Infinito's reading of Foucault, education itself is a process of ethical self-creation.

The creative aspect of power may be particularly helpful for my purposes here, if the critique of disciplinary power suggests that individuals have no choice but to be subjugated to the constraints imposed upon them. A Foucauldian self suggests otherwise, because resistance is always possible. In his later writing, Marshall (2001) explains, Foucault continued to de-emphasize the repressive aspects of power. He placed less emphasis on the repression of the self in social institutions and greater emphasis on resistance and the ways in which the self is constituted.

We need to remain careful, however, not to assume that in each individual situation, there is a correct decision to be made, some sort of ideal, freedom-forming decision. As we have seen in previous chapters, power relations in Foucault's formulation are much more contingent than that, and for this reason turning to Foucault is particularly promising. For Foucault, resistance carries no guarantees of authenticity or progress. To address Foucault's formulation of resistance requires an understanding of his concept of the self as an actor who exercises power, resists domination, and acquiesces in power relations. For Foucault, through each exercise of power, individuals continually constitute themselves.

Social self-constitution

Particularly significant for education, this Foucauldian self is open to and develops through relationships with others (Infinito, 2003). As such, social engagement is a significant part of the constitution of the self (Marshall, 2001). As Marshall (2001) states:

> the self is constituted in a pedagogical relationship with Others, and as one learns how to constitute and control the self one also learns about Others and care of others in the practices of freedom. There is a very complex interrelation of dependence between the self and others, which starts as a mentor relationship and continues with mentoring relationships. (p. 86)

In his own words, Foucault (1986/1984) speaks of the importance of social institutions for the constitution of the self in Ancient Greece:

> Around the care of the self, there developed an entire activity of speaking and writing in which the work of oneself on oneself and communication with others were linked together . . . it constituted, not an exercise in solitude . . . within more or less institutionalized structures. (p. 51)

Opening oneself to others is part of this process (Infinito, 2003), as is seeking mentors (Foucault, 1986/1984).

Another social aspect of subject constitution is the significance of engagement with radically different others, particularly those speaking with transgressive and marginalized voices (Biesta, 1998; Marshall, 2001). As Infinito (2003) explains, such engagement can result in significant, disruptive experiences that help selves critique and reconstitute themselves. Further, these engagements suggest the value of pedagogical practices in which students' taken-for-granted assumptions are disrupted, they are confronted with their ignorance, and they may be able to rethink themselves as being in a position to engage in self-creation.

Overall, the call to a Foucauldian notion of a self is a call for continual, focused reflection upon one's choices. "Foucault . . . prods us to recognize what it means or, better, what it takes, to lead ethical lives; lives distinguished by the continuous responsibility to choose ourselves through what we actually do, not the programs or the ideologies we subscribe to" (Pignatelli, 2002, p. 166). Leading ethical lives is the constant challenge, a challenge to resist normalizing practices, attending always to the ways in which one's relations with others are exercises of power.

The Crisis of the educated self

Pignatelli (2002) describes what is lost with the notion of an authentic self and the implications for ethics:

> Foucault rejects an ethics predicated upon authenticity because it leads to the subsequent assertion of veritable, timeless truths about humankind:

a modernist project that breeds certitude, complacency, and uniformity about the ethical practice. (p. 160)

The notion of a nonessential self should be devastating to the overreaching use of the standardized test and more importantly should provide ways for mounting resistance. A theory of the self is a fundamental aspect of any philosophy of education, an articulation that provides the sets of assumptions about the meaning and value of education, both as an institutional phenomenon in the form of schooling and as a cultural phenomenon in the form of socialization and nonformal education. In contrast to Foucault's formulation of self-constitution and the care of the self, the normalizing tendencies of high-stakes accountability policy represent profound constraint.

Educational theorists who have explored Foucault's notion of the self have concerned themselves with addressing issues similar to the crisis of the educated self, primarily focusing on questions about human freedom, in particular the extent to which the Foucauldian self is free to act—both as an educator and as a student. This question has led theorists to focus on projects of resistance—what remains possible to speak of in terms of free and intentioned action in light of Foucault's articulation of the normalizing power of institutions such as the public school.

At least two projects of the constitution of the self (or "projects of the self" to simplify) are relevant for resistance to normalization. These two are modified forms of critical reflection (as vigilance against subjugation) and intersubjective engagement (through social relations). These are not necessarily separate projects, although theorists are by no means of one mind about their relation to each other or about how successfully they see Foucault addressing each project.

Vigilance against subjugation, toward a social praxis

Instead of the self being constantly vigilant about being authentic, a project of the modern self (Infinito, 2003), the first and most fundamental project of the Foucauldian self is constant vigilance of a different kind; it is what Marshall (2001) describes as being "constantly vigilant against ever dangerous forms of subjugation or domination" (p. 77). A stance of "thoughtful disobedience" involves the self in constant reflection and constant change, in short, a continual exercise of freedom: "For Foucault, freedom must be continuously exercised if it is not to be lost" (Marshall, 2001, p. 77).

Infinito (2003) addresses what I term the crisis of the educated self when she "disavows" what she names as an "impoverished, subjugated self," a self imposed upon oneself from the outside, which she characterizes as being exemplified in the subject positions of many of her undergraduate teacher education students. These imposed limits are particularly dangerous for the ways in which they constrain our openness (as educators) to relationships with others, and more to the point, to the ways in which we might "transgress the given, to create ourselves as something 'other'" (p. 71).

For Infinito, the Foucauldian self has been particularly relevant for her students who, encumbered by a received notion of themselves, seem to lack capacity for understanding and caring for others who are different from themselves. This has been particularly true for her white students, who she finds to "have not been active participants in their own formation" (p. 71) and who find it difficult to relate to students of color. As participants in their own subjugation, these students not only lack experience but the "*willingness* to change . . ., to liberate themselves from imposed and unreflective being" (p. 71, emphasis in original). Without reflection, subjects contribute to their own subjugation.

To force reflection, Infinito (2003) fashions a disruptive pedagogical exercise, adapted from Jane Elliot's "Blue-Eyed, Brown-Eyed" exercise, wherein students with blue eyes are segregated and purposely subjugated, silenced, and disciplined in what Infinito describes to them as an experiment. Infinito jars her students into an emotional experience, and in the processing of the exercise she gets them to reflect upon their ethical decision making during the exercise. Using Foucault, Infinito invites struggle in her students: "Who one is and who one might become are produced mainly out of one's struggles. Yet, it is only when we consider our struggles (that which we are resistant to), that we move into a free space" (p. 75). The intention of the exercise is critical reflection so that possibilities for future action might be brought into consideration. Infinito explains concisely how she believes the exercise fosters care of the self:

Of course, it is not until we enact these future possibilities that we can be said to have transformed our existence and thus changed the world, but it is through our experiment and the communal reflection that we are "brought into being"—a being that is fundamentally ethical. (p. 75)

Self-formation happens within inescapable relations of power; it is not evaluated in terms of a projected consequence, moral principle, or virtue (in contrast to conventional Western ethics). Nor is intention most important. Instead, self-formation is the subjectivity formed in day-to-day life or, in the context of schooling, through day-to-day interactions between educators and students. Zembylas (2003) puts it this way: "self-formation is constituted *through* the power relations and the resistances that the self reshapes through performances that create greater freedom" (p. 125), while the freedom Zembylas speaks of is itself a project and "never fully coherent" (p. 113).

Similar concerns led to Infinito's observation of the crucial role of education as a form of social praxis, her observation that "the locus of ethical activity is not the mind, nor even the will, but rather in the critical and creative capacities brought forth in social praxis" (p. 73). An ethics of action, a practice with intention and reflection, engages educators in expressing and building their own "critical and creative capacities," modeling this social praxis for students, and creating educational experiences to bring forth students' capacities.

Intersubjective engagement

The second part of the project of the self, intersubjective engagement, can be taken as a critique of the limitations of critical reflection, which may be associated with forms of individualism, which for Foucault is inadequate for the constitution of the self (Marshall, 2001). Marshall is clear that Foucault warns against self-serving and narcissistic caring of the self, characteristics which we might be tempted to assign his notion of the care of the self, considering that the phrase "care of the self" may connote pampering, protecting, and luxuriating oneself, particularly at the expense of others. Foucault (1986/1984) speaks historically of how Ancient Greeks manifested this emphasis on care of the self in social relations and institutional arrangements. In a time with greater emphasis on the care of the self, social institutions served a purpose of contributing to care of the self. Foucault implies that our historical era makes it difficult to care for the self; in our historic era, structures are in place that serve other projects of the self, projects that promote individualism, for instance.

In our current context, our highly normalized notion of the self is not aligned well with the care of the self. It is possible that we do not have the institutions in place that would reinforce care of the self as a project. However, as Foucault explains these institutions, it suggests that the Ancient Greeks enjoyed many of the same social institutions we have currently, but they placed greater emphasis in some areas rather than others.

For example, in the third volume of *The History of Sexuality,* Foucault (1986/1984) goes into detail about the social institution of mentoring in this regard. One seeks "another person in whom one recognized an aptitude for guidance and counseling" (p. 53). Mentoring was a well-respected duty and in cases of existing relationships, caring for the self and for the other enriched the relationship and was reciprocated: "The care of the self appears therefore as intrinsically linked to a 'soul service,' which includes the possibility of a round of exchanges with the other and a system of reciprocal obligations" (p. 54).

Paraphrasing Foucault (1986/1984), we need others in order to take responsibility for ourselves (p. 53). Particularly important, it seems, is for mentors (and other significant others) to help us identify ways in which our actions contribute to our own subjugation and the subjugation of others. Because the Greeks placed so much emphasis on care of the self and had institutions in place to support that project, and because in the United States, not similarly interested in the care of the self and lacking institutions that would support it, the project of normalization is dominant and difficult to resist, supported through instrumental institutions and isolating social arrangements.

Taking the care of the self forward

To resist normalization is to take on a project of the care of the self. A Foucauldian notion of the care of the self, characterized by critical reflection in the form of social praxis (as vigilance against subjugation) and intersubjective engagement (through social relations) may provide promising directions for responding to the crisis of the self brought about by the constraints of high-stakes accountability. Practicing the care of the self and cultivating the conditions for promoting care of the self are the most defensible approaches for teaching, teacher education, administrator preparation, and educational policy in our current context of creeping normalization. Resisting a modernist phenomenon like normalization requires thinking differently about the educated self and imagining what we might accomplish if we were not so tied to taken-for-granted assumptions about what we as educators are supposed to be doing. Foucault proposes a view of the self that is a fundamental critique of the very nature of the modern self. Foucault's self is dynamic and not static, constituted and not discovered (Marshall, 1996).

How are we to make use of this insight? How might we take these insights to rethink the position of Iris? It may be difficult to say much about the situation Iris faces, but in the brief story that we have about her, we can already imagine some ways in which she is engaged as a professional in a somewhat limited manner and that the conditions under which she works seem to work against her philosophical position that she is responsible not for a special education classroom but for all of the individuals in that room. Her individual commitment to them seems like a tremendously promising place from which to find out more about her ethical practice, the limits she sees, and what she does when ethics come in contact with those limits. She tells us nothing about the ways in which the special education teachers support each other or even how the supervisors cultivate professional practice, her comments about threats intriguing us about potential contradictions in how special education is being pursued. These are at the very least alerts to the specific dangers of expecting children in special education, including those considered to be five grade levels behind their age-level peers, to somehow be all at the same grade level. Not only can threatening special education teachers not be a promising strategy for expanding students' proficiency, but it could not possibly be a condition under which care of the self can proliferate. Clearly resistance of some sort is called for, both personally and collectively.

The care of the self amounts to a departure from our tradition of public schooling and toward focusing attention on how individuals many cultivate themselves. In order to foster the care of the self in an institution such as a public school, which has long been embedded in modernist notions of the self, it appears that in order to foster vigilance against subjugation and intersubjective engagement, we need to consider two major areas of focus: individual and social ways to engage the care of the self. In addition to a new ethics, new institutional practices and social arrangements are needed to support the new ethics. I address these two areas in the last two chapters.

7

Educator professionalism: the active, ethical, and resistant

In search of resistance: three educators, in their own words

The following are examples of three educators' responses to questions about accountability and resistance in their schools. They represent distinct viewpoints about the ways in which high-stakes accountability policy has affected their practice.

Carol Trent

Carol Trent is a veteran math teacher at Arrowhead High School in a high-performing suburban district in Oklahoma that competes with other high-performing districts in academics and athletics. Interviewed in the Spring of 2004, Carol told her interviewer about the ways in which the state's new accountability system was causing some discord in her school between the principal and the teachers. A veteran of the school for about 10 years at the point of her interview, Carol teaches Calculus to juniors and seniors and talked with the interviewer about the math teachers' consternation about a newly adopted technology-based math curriculum. The following are noncontinuous statements from the interview:

> **Carol:** I'm in a school district that is considered a wealthy district by Oklahoma standards. We have fantastic facilities and an awful lot of time we spend trying to look good. . . . Overall, we tend to minimize the academic picture. Not in all aspects but overall. I've been involved this year in implementing a technology-based curriculum. Most of the teachers working with the implementation are very unhappy with the lack of rigor, the lack of really useful mathematics, and often even bad or incorrect mathematics in the program. . . . The Counselor's view was [that] this must be a really good program, because for the first in many years we have very few complaints from students and parents about the Algebra II program. So I'm concerned that we will judge a curriculum by the complaints received from students and parents, rather than the mathematics that's trying to be taught in that curriculum. I've notified the curriculum specialist as well as the secondary superintendent [that] some problems are just flat wrong. And it's met with kind of a shrug of the shoulder. He said, "Well, we have to supplement that."

> **Carol:** We probably are short changing our students in an effort to treat them more as consumers who have to be pleased with a product. To [some] extent, I think our students and our parents have to be confident that the education opportunities we are providing are sound. But on the other hand, I am the one who is certified to teach math and it is my responsibility to know where these students need to go. And it should be my responsibility to set the goals for the courses as I interpret them for either state standards, national standards or from observation and talking/visiting with professors at OSU and OU [Oklahoma State University and the University of Oklahoma] from their math departments.

> **Carol:** The teachers are frustrated. The teachers that I talked to are very frustrated right now. They feel pretty much across the building like we're being held accountable for fail rates that are interpreted as too high and not [listened to] when we try to explain or justify or not given credit for what we do try to do. Right now there's a bit of morale problem with the teachers. They feel the administrators are not looking at the whole picture, but just expecting the teachers to be able to fix the problems. And some teachers have talked and agreed that there will be no more "Fs." There will be no more than 10 percent of my "Fs." I don't care what I have to do to change the grades. I am not getting called in and chewed out anymore.

> **Carol:** Sometimes we do things and don't tell him. Like when we supplemented the curriculum. We just pulled out the books and just do it.

Carol: Faculty meetings are worthless. They are a waste of time. We are not ever allowed to discuss anything controversial. Communication is totally artificial versus superficial. When I told the principal at that last meeting that we lack respect, I was really putting it on the line. That is a comment that in some situations he would take extreme offense to. But I think he realized that something had to be done.

When we are in need of a situation with the administration we are not allowed to contradict them. For instance, I was told in a math teacher's luncheon with the principal last year that all engineering students—and the word "all" was used—all engineering students at OU and OSU require remedial math. That's a lie and that's what I said, which was not the most politically correct way to make that statement.

I was called down later and told I was disrespectful, that there was no way he could have known that the information was not correct. He got that information from the superintendent, and he believed that he was accurate. [Then I told him,] "You could have picked up one of our graduates that has gone into engineering that wouldn't have needed mediation on this. Several have been National Merit Scholars from the previous year." He said, "I have no way of knowing that!" He refused to admit that he could possibly be wrong. So the information still stands as far as he is concerned. I learned not to disagree with him in public.

Carl Castillo

Carl Castillo is the principal of Riverside Middle School in a working-class school district in Pennsylvania, a former mill town that now has a mixture of middle-income and low-income families. Carl describes the community as falling midway between the poorest and the richest in the state. In his interview in February 2008, he spoke extensively about the politics of education—inside his building, between districts, and at the state level. As a relatively new principal, he told us that his first task at the middle school was to establish his presence as a leader and disciplinarian. He has tried site-based management and instructional leadership and is not yet comfortable with either of those approaches to leadership. His approach is to combine availability, a positive morale, and firmness. The following are noncontinuous excerpts from his interview:

Carl: Visibility is much more of an effective strategy at the middle school level, because you're able to be proactive as opposed to reactive. You go and talk to the kids anywhere in the building and you say, "Mr. Castillo—how often do you see him?" "Man, he pops out of anywhere. He's behind plants. He's in stairwells." I mean, you do it in a joking way. Sometimes you'll hide behind a corner but then other times you're out in the open. That's my philosophy. . . . But I believe in being proactive. Keeps everybody on their toes. At the same token—you know, as a classroom teacher, if I [know] my principal could walk past my room at any minute, that may motivate me to be a little bit higher quality teacher and keep the kids actively engaged and learn. So, it's like I said, everything has a strategic purpose.

Carl: Once again, [the word is] accountability. Regardless of their personal opinions, we've got to play the game. That's what we've got to do. And I think there's a buy in on that. Because no one wants to open up the newspaper and see that your school is bad and you're a teacher there.

Carl: I saw some good things out of [NCLB] because it forces school districts and myself as a teacher to focus on subgroups of kids that just weren't measuring up. And it forces you to ask the question why. Why are these specific subgroups not measuring up? Now, we can make excuses and say it's because they're from low income families or they don't have both parents at home or wherever, but the same part is—well, what can [we] do to tackle these issues? If that's the true issue, if that's the reason why, then what can be done to try and accommodate those situations? And I think a lot of stuff has been done in the most recent years because of that. Now, once again, going back to my earlier point, a more affluent school district's going to have less subgroups because typically they're more homogenous, they're less diverse. The IEPs probably remain somewhat consistent. But an economically disadvantaged subgroup is not going to be found in a more affluent community.

Carl: "You've got to be careful with resis [voice trails off]. The more you resist the less you can do. And you're going to find yourself—you know, there's some pretty big ramifications for not making AYP. Whether you're on school improvement, whether or not there's corrective action, whether or not your job or your certification could be lost. So, you've got to play the game. You can't make the rules all the time.

Bryan Tennyson

Bryan Tennyson is principal of Olympus High School, a Pennsylvania high school that achieves very highly in the state's accountability program. As he describes his district, about 80 percent of his students' parents are professionals, and a sizable portion of the rest of his population comes from a working-class community. When interviewed in March 2010, Olympus was in the process of developing a global citizenship initiative for its high school students, a certificate program that students can voluntarily enroll in to develop a more expansive, international perspective. Teachers are leading the effort to craft an interdisciplinary curriculum that will give students opportunities inside and outside the class to appreciate how they are connected with the rest of the world and give them a chance, as Bryan says, "to take ownership of their learning." The following is one continuous excerpt from that interview:

Interviewer: *How do you see the [global citizenship initiative to be] in line with the state standards?*

Bryan: I always hope that anything we're doing is well above the state standards because the state standards tend to be minimum competencies for learning. So what I'm hoping is the things that we're doing are far exceeding what the state standards are, so we might not be covering the volumes of content that the standards often, you know, assume that they can cover, but hopefully we're gaining a much richer and deeper academic perspective and a much richer and deeper development of skills than what the state standards would call for.

Interviewer: *So you don't really see much problem with it—with the fact that sometimes developing programs in social sciences are kind of tough because they're not that much tested, so sometimes it's kind of tough to find a rationale for it, but you don't think that would be a problem here?*

Bryan: Well, we're always going to probably in some way have to bend to the test of the day, or whether it's the PSSA for now, and it's the Keystone Exams to come. As long as those tests are high stakes for kids, and they're high stakes for schools, we're always going to have to respect and prepare students for that. Because it's obviously important to their future from a high stakes standardized testing perspective. But I don't think that means that you exclude all the other richer, deeper parts of education, and I don't think you have to. I mean if you're talking about a certain topic and you're introducing other perspectives, that doesn't—that shouldn't then make the content any less rich, or any less important, or for the student to have to know any less content. So I think there's a way that it can be done, and hopefully if you give a richer and deeper view of something they'll actually be better able to understand the content, or they'll be more passionate to want to learn it because you're trying to make the overall lesson more engaging and more relevant for the students. I think it certainly can be done.

Putting the self to work

In their comments about how high-stakes accountability policy has affected their schools and their practices, the words of Carol Trent, Carl Castillo, and Bryan Tennyson help map the landscape of resistance to the dangers associated with high-stakes accountability policy. Each is in a position of attempting to take charge of his or her own professionalism. While Carol is located in a well-positioned school district, she is experiencing the beginnings of pressure from her principal, who Carol positions as being more interested in test scores and complying with state mandates than a rigorous curriculum that would hold up to what she terms to be more meaningful accountability: how well students are prepared to succeed at college-level math. Carol and her colleagues feel their professionalism eroding away, and they are struggling with various forms of overt and covert resistance to hold their ground.

As principals, Carl and Bryan represent distinctly different contexts within the same Pennsylvania county. Both men are relatively new principals, but they have different orientations toward the politics of resistance under high-stakes accountability. Carl comes across as primarily political in his orientation and willing to adjust practice for the sake of compliance. Something is holding him back, and it is unclear whether it is modest capacity in the district, his own discomfort with instructional leadership, or the extent of the challenge.

In contrast to both situations, Bryan, who leads the high school in a district considered to be one of the highest performing in the state (a position that Carol's district holds in her state), comes across as more confident and grounded in a belief that the goal of high standards supersedes compliance. His resistance to a constricted curriculum helps him facilitate a teacher-directed reform of a global citizenship program, something that will not be captured on any high-stakes test, but the confidence with which he asserts his belief makes it seem not like resistance at all.

In the last chapter, I came to the conclusion that resisting normalization should take the form of the care of the self, a Foucauldian ethics of possibility that requires educators to engage in individual and social praxis. In what follows, I build a relational theory of professionalism from the basis of the care of the self. In this chapter, I define an active/ethical framework conceptually and describe how it may address the philosophical and ethical difficulties presented by high-stakes accountability policy. The active/ethical project is a positive and affirming project, but I cannot get away from the fact of its resistance to what may be the easier course to take or to what others encourage, reward, or believe to be possible. The active/ethical professional rethinks the position of educator as receiver of dictates and instead acts as informed, creative, and morally grounded.

In this chapter, I argue for these three tenets of professionalism for educators:

1. **As a professional, an educator is in a position to profess substantive beliefs about the meaning and value of education.** In other words,

a professional educator has a philosophy of education and engages others who may have different ideas about the meaning and value of education. A philosophy of education grounded on the care of the self is a philosophy of possibility.

2. **As a professional, an educator is in a position to exercise ethical and professional judgment.** An educator is in a position to continually develop ethical and professional judgment throughout his career and in his various positions of responsibility. Further, professional judgment spans the positions of educators throughout the educational sector. Active/ethical professionalism applies to PreK-12 educators, school leaders, school boards, teacher educators, graduate educators, and policymakers.

3. **As a professional, an educator is in a position to acknowledge and resist opportunities to enact normalization on herself, students, and colleagues.** One very important part of articulating an active/ethical professionalism is being clear on the role that resistance plays in order to achieve more defensible educational aims than those that are encouraged by high-stakes accountability policy. To act ethically, an educator needs to understand how and why her work must at some level be resistant.

In this chapter I engage these three parts in greater detail. The first part is to describe how the care of the self may translate into a philosophy of education that works against normalization. The second part is a bridging section on the importance of ethical and professional judgment and cultivating it among educators. The third part is a longer section, a more extended treatment on how we might define resistance in a manner that is effective for a broad array of educators, not just those who find resistance a natural thing to do.

I am well aware that many educators are very uncomfortable thinking of themselves as resistant. There are lingering concerns in their reluctance to be resistant that look quite similar to the common concerns that educators and scholars have had to the educational lessons in Foucault's *Discipline and Punish*. Engaging the concept of normalization may seem both negative and futile. The danger of focusing an ethical framework on "resistance" is that the active/ethical framework may appear to be merely reactive to the conditions that others establish or it is designed to avoid pitfalls rather than a project that has form itself. Educators dealing with the normalization associated with high-stakes accountability policy are unlikely to find a stance of mere resistance very satisfying.

Thinking differently needs to be more than critical; creative forms of action are needed. And so for these reasons, I consciously position my approach as simultaneously active and ethical. I want educators to be actively working as educators from a position of reasoned, robust ethicality. To do so, however, they need to become comfortable with the ways in which their work is resistant. Mostly I want educators to think of themselves as resistant to structures and regimes of truth that would have them normalize themselves and normalize others, including students, parents, and each other.

Foucault himself wrote very little about resistance and even less about resistance in educational practice, and so the Foucault scholarship has taken resistance on as a project of extending Foucault's published work. For this purpose, I turn to a formulation of "critical resistance" by David Couzens Hoy (2004), who considers Foucault and other critical and post-structural theorists in a post-critical frame. While Hoy does not address accountability policy or education, he provides multiple ways for imagining aspects of resistance that might be responsive to the domination and normalization associated with high-stakes accountability. Hoy is concerned that resistance not be conceptualized as entirely reactive, for instance, and like the educational philosophers using Foucault's work to theorize resistance, Hoy is concerned that a notion of resistance be clear on action. Along with Hoy, I wish to argue that in the face of normalization, we are called to attend to *ethical resistance* as well as *social/political resistance*.

For the active/ethical professional, what is the desired educated self?

From the previous chapter, the care of the self emerges as an engaged self, continually constituted through relations with others, mindful of exercises of power, both positive and negative, open to possibility, and attendant to difference. How might this self form the basis for a philosophy of education? It should be relevant for engaging the various swirling conversations around us that advance varied ideas about the aims of education or help us deal with times when aims talk is set aside in favor of a default philosophy of education to inhabit educational practice. If we are open to possibilities across difference, mindful of hidden possibilities, and vigilant against oppressive power relations, we can open space for open-ended aims for education. The constituting self with limited opportunities for exploring possibilities is limited in its pursuit of freedom, although as Foucault makes it clear, in every relation the individual has an opportunity to reflect upon its situation and ponder alternatives.

As I explained in Chapter 5, in *Discipline and Punish,* Foucault (1995/1975) is clear that a desirable but constraining aspect of the modern self is that individuals discipline themselves through technologies of the self, participating in their own subjection (Foucault, 1995/1975). As I explained in Chapter 6, when Foucault takes up the problem of the modern self again in *The Hermeneutics of the Subject* (2005/2001), one gets a clearer sense that while Foucault embraces the modernist desires for seeking freedom and truth, he finds the modern notion of the self to be limited in contrast to the views of the Ancient Greeks. After what he calls the Cartesian moment, the modern self accesses truth through the acquisition of knowledge:

> I think the modern age of the history of truth begins when knowledge itself and knowledge alone gives access to the truth. That is to say, it is when the philosopher (or the scientist, or simply someone who seeks the truth) can recognize the truth and have access to it in himself and solely through his activity of knowing, without anything else being demanded of him and without him having to change or alter his being as subject. (p. 17)

Descartes' rationality and epistemology (a theory of knowledge, its definition and basis for justification) is at issue here, the predecessor to subsequent modernist views of knowledge as ascertainable by the knowing subject, whether through deduction, perception, or experience. Foucault names the link to education in such a view of the self: "to have access to the truth we must have studied, have an education, and operate within a certain scientific consensus" (p. 18). We might term this view of the modern self a modernist exemplar, since in the modern tradition there are multiple examples of philosophers who do not limit the search for truth just to the propositional knowledge Foucault speaks of in this passage.

Foucault acknowledges the Aristotelian tradition as an exception. While the view excerpted evokes logical positivism (the source of the verification principle whereby knowledge is limited to that which can be empirically verified), social scientists have largely rejected the verification principle and turned to various alternative theoretical perspectives, including post-positivism, following Karl Popper (1963, 1994/1965). Post-positivism, which informs the work of psychometricians who design standardized tests, takes on a probabilistic and fallibilistic view of knowledge after Popper and attempts to account for the very distortions Foucault speaks of.

Significantly, Foucault departs from this view for the status it gives the knowing subject and for its limiting the search of truth to the epistemological and the underlying objectivist version thereof. Other theoretical perspectives, including interpretivism and social constructionism (Crotty, 1998; Paul, 2005), might be said to be different from Foucault's formulation to the extent that they retain the modernist notion of the knowing subject and the distinction mentioned above between propositional knowledge and other forms of knowing.

Nevertheless, this modernist view characterizes a view of the self and knowledge perpetuated by high-stakes accountability policy, for one would have to believe in just such a view of the self, knowledge, and truth to willfully grant standardized tests the authority they receive currently in public education. If teaching to the test, narrowing the curriculum to tested subject areas, and aligning instruction to standardized texts, tests and outcomes (Sirotnik, 2004) were one's educational philosophy, one would have to believe that the educated self is achieved primarily through the acquisition of testable knowledge. One would have to be a thoroughgoing logical positivist, and it is doubtful that the logical positivists would even have agreed to such a characterization of education or the self.

If an educated self is one capable of seeking "truth," then surely Foucault's more expansive notion of truth is called for, making for a more integrated notion of the self (I would prefer a different word than "truth," one that does not carry the modernist connotation of "truth" that Foucault is trying to get away from). Following Foucault, we have the basis for conceptualizing education as a project of the care of the self—selfhood as continually constituting and open to possibility, but ever vigilant and resistant to normalizing tendencies. Alternative educational philosophies and models of the educated self need to remain in play, such as discourses about the meaning and value of the arts and arts instruction. Further, educators need to appreciate the value of standards and curricula but also be aware of state standards and curricula as contested and historically situated documents, socially constructed and necessarily excluding some subject matter and aspects of self-constitution. Educators need to be aware of the roles that discourses play in governing our actions, and they need to act to keep alternative discourses alive, even when they seem to run counter to prevailing norms.

For example, it is a challenge to disentangle the goals of high standards and the normalizing practices that those goals authorize. There is a strong sense in which the use of standards has not only contributed to the deleterious, "unintended" effects of high-stakes accountability, but also the argument may be made that pushing the notion of high standards is paradoxically oppressive for its taking for granted a fixed notion of the self. The processes that lead to the creation of standards, as Popkewitz (1991) and Jan Masschelein and Maarten Simons (2005) argue, mask the various necessary exercises of power that occur when committees and commissions decide what subject matter to include and exclude. These processes that Popkewitz and Masschelein and Simons describe, wherein representatives are asked to participate in the construction of standards, provide the illusion of participation and democratic action, paradoxically involving teachers in their own mode of subjection (Foucault, 1990/1976).

When high stakes are attached to high standards, the "unintended" effects spin out of control. Hastily prepared standards add more content to grade level curricula than students performing below grade level can handle, discouraging teachers who cannot fit in all the standards in the amount of time they have, encouraging schools and districts to develop pacing guides so that all standards are covered, encouraging teachers to cover material too quickly. Having standards in place for the sake of complying with NCLB is counterproductive.

A philosophy of education based on the care of the self should provide robust alternatives to pacing guides, enable teachers to prioritize standards, and work across grade levels to take ownership of the whole curriculum across subject matter, modes of being, and grade level. The value of an education based on the care of the self is that students have the opportunity to constitute themselves in multiple fashions and in relation to a wide variety of subject matter and modes of being.

Ethical and professional judgment

The second tenet of professionalism is ethical and professional judgment. The distrust of teachers' judgment and ability to assess student progress without standardized measures is a widespread phenomenon, especially in relation to teachers in target schools, quite often urban districts. In the research literature and in my observations in various research studies, well-positioned schools are more likely to have environments which allow teachers leeway in developing curriculum, instruction, and assessment. Mathison and Freeman (2003) articulate ways in which professional judgment and school or district policy are at odds, when high-stakes accountability challenges the better judgment of educators, who find themselves engaging in means-ends bargains with themselves:

> The teachers at Hemlock and Willow Elementary Schools are not radicals. They do not seek complete autonomy, they do not challenge the need for accountability (even bureaucratic accountability), they find some virtue in state mandated tests, they are content within centralized systems that proscribe many aspects of their work. But, they also perceive themselves as professionals with both the responsibility and capability of doing their jobs well and in the best interests of their students. (p. 19)

As I mentioned previously, the teachers Mathison and Freeman studied often find themselves preparing their students to do well on high-stakes tests, despite their beliefs that their instruction is miseducative and counterproductive to student learning.

When teachers exercise their judgment or act against their judgment of what is most educative, they are exercising power, without clarity about who or what exactly is influencing them and whose interests they are serving. But that is how Foucauldian power is exercised—in the small, day-to-day decisions that support larger power apparatuses (Pignatelli, 1993). The study of the local, day-to-day power relations, what has come to be called the micropolitical, is significant for the educator searching for means of everyday resistance. In the micropolitical context, power relations play out in relationships. Mayo (2000) describes what is at stake:

> to the degree that one's relationships have power effects, one must interrogate those relationships, as well as one's relationship to oneself. While one's position and one's relationships are not ever going to be outside of power, they may be reconfigured into new, less problematic ones. (p. 115)

Micropolitical analysis helps us to see ethics in all educational interactions. Resistance to normalization requires greater attention to ethics in the relations we cultivate. This ethical project is the centerpiece of Foucault's notion of the care of the self, and it is echoed in Freire's (2005/1997) contention about what is basic to the development of an educator as a professional: "It is important that we take critical ownership of the formation of our selves" (p. 44). The notion of the care of the self provides educators with a complex sense of the moral nature of their practice—what Infinito (2003) terms ethical self-formation. Rarely are the ethical aspects of teaching cultivated, reinforced, or considered fundamental to educational practice, but the care of the self places them at the center of educational practice.

The ethical development of professionals is tied to cultivation of professional judgment at all levels in education—fostering it in educators, expecting it, and respecting it. School leaders and school boards also need to cultivate their judgment (Joseph Dietrich [2010] explains how school boards are seemingly inattentive to the ways in which they accede decision-making responsibility to the state). For example, I often hear from teachers who distrust their professional judgment about the abilities and achievements of their students in favor of test scores. (Any knowledgeable standardized test maker would advise teachers to use test scores as part of their professional judgment, not as a replacement, but teachers rarely come in contact with test makers.) If judgments about students' progress or future placement are at stake, teachers are willing to displace their own professional judgment about the efficacy of preparing children for standardized tests; they may even reason that failing to prepare children for tests would put the children at peril (Mathison & Freeman, 2003).

These educators see the real effects of poor test performance, such as grade retention or exclusion from future opportunities. These teachers are placed in the paradoxical situation of acquiescing to normalizing practices because they reason that resisting might actually constrain students' future possibilities. Whether the ends they envision would play themselves out or not is beside the point; at base, Mathison and Freeman point out, the teachers' ethical reasoning is dominated by utilitarian ethics.

As I mentioned in Chapter 3, if as utilitarians teachers act from the principle of utility (in which ethically defensible actions are those that produce the greatest good for the greatest number), even in the best of circumstances, they are bounded by their expectations of how future educational institutions will treat their students. The ultimate real school effects for their students are dependent upon institutional decisions (cutoff scores and the design of the tests, for example). The teachers may lack faith that the future institutional decisions about grade promotion (if the child performed inadequately on the standardized test) would be in the best interest of the children. Furthermore, within the existing institutional and social arrangements, alternatives are limited. In this example, these elementary teachers are placed in an institutionally created dilemma, with no clearly evident choice that is ethically defensible. Taken in isolation, the situation itself is intractable without transforming the context and reformulating the discursive practices at play.

Preparing educators for resistance

In the current public school context, it is difficult to avoid acquiescence and enact resistance. While we wait for alternative educational policies that are more democratic and more equitable, educators need to take charge of their own professionalism. Regardless of the state, national, or district policies, educators are still responsible for their day-to-day ethical and professional responses to students, parents, and their colleagues. Regardless of what form the next reauthorization of ESEA takes, the structures and regimes of truth that NCLB set into place will still have their influence. What kind of resistance is needed so educators can configure themselves as responsible in a more robust and educationally defensible manner that what is demanded through external accountability systems?

In this section I look to varied conceptions of resistance with the aim of explaining how resistance might most helpfully be incorporated into active/ethical professionalism. A robust and everyday resistance is needed, all the more so because of how educators are positioned in multiple relations of power—as adults in positions to discipline and be disciplined, to normalize and be normalized, and to resist and be resisted. Educators at all levels—teachers, principals, superintendents, and other educators and administrators—need help resisting the normalizing technologies authorized by high-stakes accountability policy, not only the legally mandated procedures, such as sanctions for low-performing schools and graduation tests and preferences granted to experimental research and scripted curriculum. Also significant are the exercises of power that people make in response to policy in various sites—states, school districts, schools, and classrooms. As I explained before, these ancillary exercises of power effect a reversal of power of the technology of the examination, in Foucault's (1995/1975) terms, and further normalizing and discipline, reaching to the point of self-discipline, self-surveillance, and redeployment of spectacle (Vinson & Ross, 2003).

Resistance in pedagogy

But first, to scout out the ground of resistance in education, I revisit some older work by Maxine Greene (1988) and Henry Giroux (1988, 1991; Giroux & McLaren, 1988). At around the same time, in the years after *A Nation at Risk,* Giroux and Greene each lay out the ideals for a project of resistance for professional educators. In their works, they imagine emancipatory roles for educators while working through the limitations and challenges that power relations present for enacting them. I have chosen them as representative of discourses that resonate particularly well with my proclivities toward philosophies of education embedded in creative self creation (Greene, 1988; Otto, 2000) and critical, pro-feminist, and anti-racist pedagogy (Ellsworth, 1989, 1997; Freire, 2000/1970; Giroux, 1988; hooks, 1994; Kumashiro, 2004). My aim here is not to present these as the only philosophies of education that are compatible with a Foucauldian ethic, but to show how ethical resistance drawn from Foucault helps round out a comprehensive philosophical and ethical approach to education.

Greene is a philosopher of education who has written extensively on the aesthetic and existential value of educational experience. In the 1960s, Greene's philosophy broke from the analytic philosophical emphasis in which most of her peers were writing at the time to make better use of existentialism and literary tradition. The most committed and respected advocate for the value of the arts and aesthetic experience in the education of all children, Greene is described by Michelle Fine (2010) as "*a social movement with thousands of grandchildren*" (p. xvii, *italics in original*) and by Kathy Hytten (2010) as a practitioner of "engaged philosophy" and "embodied scholarship" (p. 22). Greene draws from the literary, modern humanist, existentialist, and postmodern traditions to argue for purpose in education that centers the creative and agentic capacities of individuals (Noddings, 2010).

In *The Dialectic of Freedom,* Greene (1988) is concerned with a project of naming the limits on freedom of educational reform that began brewing in the 1980s and which, if we follow the trail laid out by the contributors to Sirotnik's (2004) edited collection of essays on accountability, can be seen to culminate in the high-stakes accountability movement and the NCLB legislation. Greene points to the growing subjection of public schooling:

> The language of contemporary schooling . . . emphasizes something quite different . . . unable to perceive themselves in interpretive relation to it,

the young (like their elders) are all too likely to remain immersed in the taken-for-granted and the everyday. (p. 7)

Greene imagines something quite different as an aim for schooling—the pursuit of freedom—and her formulation of freedom draws on Freire's notion of human unfinishedness and Foucault's (and others') notions of the constitution of the subject and the significance of possibility. From Freire, she takes the notion of humans as subjects as opposed to objects, as "men and women in the striving toward their own 'completion'—a striving that can never end" (p. 8). The self she envisions is a self in process, an agent of its continual creation.

Similarly, Greene's idea of freedom is not determinate or utopian. Her conception of freedom comes through when she posits it as follows:

We might, for the moment, think of it as a distinctive way of orienting the self to the possible, of overcoming the determinate, of transcending or moving beyond in the full awareness that such overcoming can never be complete. (p. 5)

She also suggests that self-creation is co-extensive with the search for freedom, when she says that "It is, actually, in the process of effecting transformations that the human self is created and re-created" (p. 21). With this definition of freedom, Greene captures the hopes of resistance that critiques and also creates.

Greene (1988) addresses a few specific roles of teachers in this conception of freedom, suggesting a number of features that represent exercises of freedom. I take these up later also and mention them now as a way to begin thinking about what resistance might look like in a professional educator. One fundamental insight is the role that engagement in communities of difference plays in imagining responses to obstacles, and most significantly (and most evocative of Foucault), Greene is also concerned that promoting freedom in students is rather impossible if the teacher is not likewise engaged in his or her own project of freedom. She is concerned for the sense of responsibility for the other that comes with true freedom, drawing from Thomas Jefferson the sense in which freedom is dependent upon collaboration and mutual concern. Greene's vision of the educated self is one embedded in human dignity, continual striving, and a disposition toward unfinishedness. Her vision provides a sense of what the individual who resists is striving toward—not a transcendent vision but one of struggle and attentiveness.

Giroux provides a complementary perspective. One of the first critical theorists in education to make use of postmodern theory, Giroux is explicitly concerned with using postmodern notions of power relations to augment the modernist project of critical pedagogy. In an essay in which Giroux

(1991) elaborates his notion of border pedagogy, he explains his desire for a critical project that combines the most useful aspects of modernism and postmodernism:

> We need to combine the modernist emphasis on the capacity of individuals to use critical reason to address the issue of public life with a postmodernist concern with how we might experience agency in a world constituted in differences unsupported by transcendent phenomena or metaphysical guarantees. (p. 72)

Here Giroux expresses well the tensions that any theorist faces when he or she takes seriously the limitations of powerful theoretical concepts from critical theory, such as critical consciousness. Giroux stresses the importance of acting as an agent in a world without metaphysical guarantees—this postmodern identification implies that he will find ethics from the philosophical traditions to be inadequate. Giroux does not address ethics specifically. His concern is for social and political action, and those who argue for critical projects seldom draw from ethical theory to support the moral value of its projects. (An exception is Joe Kincheloe & Peter McLaren, 1994, who draw from Welch [1990] for an ethical basis for critical inquiry, as explored by Gunzenhauser, 1999.)

In a chapter co-written with Peter McLaren, Giroux specifically addresses resistance, and they propose counter-hegemony as a similar but alternative concept to resistance. Their move is to encourage teachers to find, uncover, or create alternatives to hegemonic constructions. This move plays out in their later work in their critiques of popular culture and their emphasis on counter-hegemonic cultural forms (Giroux, 1994, 1996, 1997, 2010). With counter-hegemony, Giroux and McLaren (1988) aim to maintain the notion of critique inherent in the concept of resistance, but more than that, to effect "new social relations and public spaces that embody alternative forms of experience and struggle" (p. 163).

Together, these pieces can be taken as the articulation of desired attributes of a critical postmodern resistance for educational practice. The framing is as border pedagogy, an evolution of critical pedagogy, responding to critical pedagogy's limitations as an enacted practice. Giroux wants to take account of desire, differential power relations between various identity groups, and the paralyzing inertia associated with mere critique. The call for counter-hegemony is a call to create the alternatives that go beyond mere critique. Giroux sets out a bold and ambitious set of desired states of affairs, arising from his basis in the philosophy of Freire, for cultivating humanity, respecting human unfinishedness, and promoting critical consciousness (Freire, 1988, 2000/1970). The ultimate service is not to Freire's notion of humanity or to Greene's term—the dialectic of freedom—but to radical democracy, drawing mostly from Chantal Mouffe for its definition.

The value of the work is the ambitious goals he lays out for redefining, rethinking, and reimagining concepts, relations, and practices. Giroux calls on critical educators to do the detail work that remains to be done (and Giroux also does so in his subsequent work). Those working in the critical pedagogy tradition advocate many strategies. Among those strategies is engaging in visual media and other forms of popular culture, getting teachers and students to interrogate meanings conveyed in these forms of culture, to engage in inquiry to understand in greater detail the structures and other cultural forms that the meanings reinforce, and to create their own media. Another project is to bring to the fore the experiences and perspectives of subjugated persons and groups. It is an effective way to teach about and against racism, for instance. The various forms of action are social and political forms of resistance, and authors have argued for ways to integrate this approach into various subject matters and grade levels.

Critical pedagogy can be an effective way to teach about normalization and to advance critique. Social and political action is also part of the project, and Vinson and Ross (2003) provide examples in relation to high-stakes accountability policy. Those inclined to social and political action tend to find the work rich and useful; they are less so for those educators less inclined to such action, those who are politically moderate or conservative, or those whose skill sets or more timid personalities do not incline them to enact the suggested strategies. Others seek more explicitly self-reflexive critical projects (Noblit et al., 2004). These educators still wish to develop themselves as professionals and to work on a day-to-day basis to resist normalization.

In the critical pedagogy tradition, it is more difficult to address alternative projects at the level of day-to-day practice and ethical relations, and examples are far less extensive. Partly that is because critical pedagogy in its more widely circulated forms draws mostly from sociological and political theory and little from ethical theory. The exception is in a related, but more philosophical discourse, for example, a project edited by Ilan Gur Ze'ev (2005). As such, there is unfinished work to connect critical pedagogy to the ethical subject acting in resistance on a daily basis.

In these early essays mentioned, while Giroux does not engage ethical theory explicitly, he does seem very interested in an ethical aspect of resistance. In the early essays, it seems that the notion of resistance Giroux proposes is ultimately self-critical, for throughout his work he wishes to avoid the dangers of reinscribing domination, not only in practices he mentions but also in his own formulations. I read Giroux here as an idealist in this sense, vigilant to the "greater danger" among the choices we make, about which Foucault speaks.

In the drive for idealistic self-critique, Giroux at this point does not yet reconfigure a theory of self in relation to the modernist elements that he wishes to maintain. On the road to radical democracy are significant iterative steps. What I mean by that is exemplified in the following passage, wherein Giroux (1991) imagines how Foucault's notion of countermemory might be put to use in border pedagogy:

> it is imperative for critical educators to develop a discourse of countermemory, not as an essentialist and closed narrative, but as part of a utopian project that recognizes "the composite, heterogeneous, open, and ultimately indeterminate character of the democratic tradition." The pedagogical issue here is the need to articulate difference as part of the construction of a new type of subject, which would be both multiple and democratic. (p. 74, citing Mouffe herein)

Unclear in this rationale for using countermemory is articulation of what he means specifically by a subject being multiple and democratic. It seems that Giroux is advocating a notion of self-constitution through engagement with difference. Democracy seems imprecise here, although it may be that the innovative possibilities are in figuring out what a democratic self would look like. Regardless, Giroux has provided a fundamentally radical notion of subject constitution here, which, at least in this quotation and in many other places in his work, is embedded in his concern for democracy. For some other theorists, notions of agency, the subject or the self hold that place. I suspect it is because Giroux's emphasis is on political/social resistance, particularly in the form of social movements. As he implies here (and states outright elsewhere in his work), politics and ethics are both needed.

Foucauldian resistance

How might we augment Greene's educational vision and Giroux's social/political resistance with a Foucauldian ethic? Would these three ideas together provide a sufficiently power-savvy resistance to normalization that would make education a project of freedom formation? To start, in light of the theories of Foucault, it is important to see the ways in which one's own day-to-day practice, enmeshed in power relations, may be creative. As Hoy (2004) says, in summarizing Foucault, "Power can be productive if it opens up new possibilities, but it turns into domination if its function becomes entirely the negative one of shrinking and restricting possibilities" (p. 66).

As Hoy explains, Foucault saw his methodological project of genealogy as a form of resistance, for through genealogy, the subject may be open to possibilities otherwise unavailable. Through a genealogical project, "We will not be able to go back to the past or to step out of our culture entirely, but we may be able to find the resources in ourselves to save ourselves from the destructive tendencies that the contrast reveals" (Hoy, 2004, p. 63). Genealogy, in other words, helps the subject to be vigilant against its own subjugation.

Similarly to Greene, Foucault is interested in ways in which a subject may be able to see possibilities that technologies of normalization would otherwise foreclose. Disciplined selves are complicit in their own subjugation when as modern subjects they comply with the procedures of self-discipline and the comparison of one's traits to social norms. As I have mentioned, teachers and administrators find themselves in multiple relations of power in this formulation. They are both normalized and normalizing, due to the constraints placed upon them, but also their positions in relation to students and each other. The need is crucial for educators to be able to see themselves in these rather complicated relations of power and the ways in which they may be complicit with subjugation.

As I have repeated, for Foucault, resistance is ever present, for power relations cannot exist without it. As Hoy explains, if it were not for the potential of resistance, there would be no need for the exercise of power. Domination is in essence an attempt to restrain resistance. In a school context, a restrictive or prescriptive curriculum, for example, subjugates to the extent that it obviates alternatives. A test regimen subjugates because it leads to restricting possibilities.

Resistance emerges from critique, with Foucault placing genealogy in a prime place for exposing the historicity of normalizing practices. In school settings, partial critiques of normalizing practices may emerge that are just as significant for resistance. Without elaborate genealogical understandings of the progression of the technology of the examination, for example, educators can launch critiques of the normalizing practices that arise in response to high-stakes accountability. Educators can tap into other possibilities; through philosophies of education and other discourses, such as those surrounding instruction in the arts, educators are daily able to identify strategies of resistance to normalization. Their opportunities may certainly be richer the more educators know the genealogy of what they are working against, the danger being that without knowing the genealogy, educators may have to rely on ad hoc resistance at every turn, which could be difficult to sustain and to connect across projects.

This ad hoc resistance may fall short, and indeed it is falling short on a daily basis. What Hoy terms as social/political resistance amounts to the marshaling of resources and institutions to change oppressive social relations (and similar to the actions that Giroux [1988, 1991] and Vinson and Ross [2003] advocate). Foucault's notion of resistance provides essential theoretical support for this form of resistance. In regard to professional practice, we need something more than moments of individual actions. We need instead something like a stance, a set of habits that places an educator in a position of constant vigilance against normalization. Hoy speaks of this by engaging Foucault and Judith Butler on the cultivation of virtue:

> If Foucault's idea of connecting the critical attitude to virtue is to reinforce the idea of practice, virtue in general would then be the result of constant attention to the habits that would build the critical attitude more deeply into our conduct. (p. 96)

Giroux's underlying notion of self-critique is particularly relevant here, but Hoy (2004) also helps us by drawing attention to what critique means for self-creation: "the point of critique is to enhance the lives and the possibilities of individuals, to allow them the space to try to create themselves as works of art" (p. 92).

Staying focused now on this notion of constant vigilance, Hoy (2004) addresses the limit work that critique necessitates:

> For Foucault, the force of critique is that the encounter with one's limits dissolves one's background belief that there are no other ways to experience the phenomena in question. Insofar as the dissolution of this background belief amounts to dissolving fundamental beliefs about oneself, it opens up other possibilities and reshapes one's sense of what can be done. Critique is thus a crucial condition of freedom. (p. 92)

Unpacking this excerpt now, we can see essential elements of the desired critical stance: the awareness of possibilities we've already identified, the challenge to one's background beliefs, a different but related aspect of self-critique, and the "sense of what can be done," implying the articulation of possible actions. We also see with these elements a reconnection to Greene and her notion of freedom.

Hoy explores an example that comes from Butler's engagement with Foucault. As Hoy explains it, Butler speaks of how the subject is at once limited and enacted by domination. She suggests that owning one's domination, redefining it, enables the subject to resist. Hoy's (2004) summary of her point:

> Only by accepting, occupying, and taking over the injurious term, says Butler, "can I resist and oppose it, recasting the power that constitutes me as the power I oppose." (p. 98, quoting Butler from *The Psychic Life of Power*)

This reinforces the utility of having educators engage their own subjection, naming the terms of their subjection and redefining them. This resistance might be imagined quite literally as redefining key terms, such as "accountability," somewhat like Sirotnik (2004) undertakes by attempting to redefine and expand it as "responsible accountability."

More so, the terms of one's subjection should come under scrutiny. Hoy (2004) sums up what he means by that:

> Virtue in general, then, would be the practice of risking one's deformation as a subject by resistance not to the constraining principles per se, but to one's attachment to them insofar as they constitute one's identity. (p. 100)

As one example, Zembylas (2003) demonstrates how educators may rethink emotional discourses to reconstitute their experiences of being normalized. In this important work, he demonstrates how teachers are affected emotionally by the value attributed (through discursive practices) to their teaching when their students do not score well on high-stakes tests. Zembylas explains how teacher education students are sometimes able to reformulate those emotions by looking for other cues of their students' participation, engagement, and learning. As he explains, this is not without struggle, and as in the following case, can take considerable time:

> after many years of unsuccessful struggle and resistance, Catherine interrupted the emotion discourse and performance of shame and frustration by capitalizing on students' excitement with her progressive approach. Performing this new discourse of excitement provided Catherine with strategies for questioning the "teaching to the test" approach and resisting the characterizations imposed on her (that she was a failure). (p. 126)

In the situation Zembylas describes, Catherine was able to reframe herself as a successful professional by paying attention to alternative indicators of student engagement and success—students' excitement—to feel more confident about her teaching, no longer letting the accountability system define her. Catherine did not let herself be normalized by the system, and she did not allow herself to continue to normalize her students. In testimony to the difficulty, Zembylas indicates that this happened after many years.

In her collection of essays, Bronwyn Davies (2000) does similar work. In one example, a collaboration with Cath Laws, the role of principal is recast against discourses that would normalize adolescent behaviors as deviant. In this essay, Laws' interactions with students demonstrate how she re-imagines disciplinary situations (and in some cases on the spot, which is all the more remarkable) that disrupt cultural themes that would distance Laws from her students. The effects are eminently richer relations, and ultimately, more expanded possibilities for Laws' future practice as an educator (when she succeeds with a student) and for the students themselves (when they have the opportunity to reconstitute themselves as agents of their own experience, rather than being subjected to disciplinary action).

Unfortunately, few educators are as skilled as Laws. As Giroux and Greene noted many years ago, educators are underprepared to negotiate their roles in the inadequate and unequal situations in which they find themselves. Teachers lack the key features of self-constitution deemed essential for the creation of humane and freedom-forming educational practices. Taking three considerations Greene mentions, we can see significant obstacles.

First, teachers lack experience engaging in communities of difference. Getting those experiences, even prior to teacher education programs, seems important; Gloria Ladson-Billings (2001) describes situations in which teacher education students who already come into their programs with experiences working with diverse communities are readily able to put those experiences to work toward greater collaboration with communities of students and parents who are different from them.

Second, as Greene (1988) notes, the teacher who is engaged in his or her own project of freedom is the teacher most likely to encourage the same in a student. As Foucault notes, the care of the self, as a project of self-constitution, relies greatly on the modeling and mentoring of care of the self. Conditions that reflect centralized control of curriculum in order to meet expectations of high-stakes accountability systems work against this. Exercises of power that accede control for curriculum and instruction to state legislatures or district offices do little to promote the educator's modeling of freedom.

Third, Greene's notion of freedom implies responsibility for the other. To engage the failings in this aspect of self-constitution in public schools, we need to turn to Hoy's notion of ethical resistance.

Ethical resistance

It is probably more difficult for educators to conceptualize what Hoy terms as ethical resistance. Particularly problematic for the context of high-stakes accountability are the changing relations between teachers and students and between teachers and parents. Recall from Chapter 4 that Biesta (1998, 2004) characterizes these changing relations as economic, arguing through the use of Bauman's notion of responsibility, pointing out an ironically decreasing public responsibility for universal education in the enactment of high-stakes accountability. Sirotnik (2004) similarly notes shifting patterns of responsibility for equitable public education away from the public and onto scapegoats.

To extend Foucault, Hoy turns to Levinas and Derrida for his discussion of ethical resistance as a way of establishing a nonfoundational basis for ethics. Ontologically prior is the ethical obligation placed upon us by the other, according to Levinas. As Hoy states, "For Levinas ethics is most primordially involved in the encounter with the *face* of the other" (p. 152).

Ethical resistance, for Levinas, is the inescapable resistance exerted by the completely powerless, the face of which never dies, amounting to "perhaps paradoxically the most powerful form that resistance can take" (p. 16).

What I take Hoy to mean by this is that the ontological connection between the self and other, characterized by one's awareness via the face of "the other as like the self but different from the self" (p. 152) as a primordial condition, provides a pull of some sort from the other not to be dominated. Resistance is somewhat like a plea from the other that cannot go answered. Hoy explains it this way:

> Instead, resistance is experienced as a summons from the other precisely not to do violence to the other. Resistance is thus fundamentally ethical, and *ethical* resistance is primordially nonviolent: "the 'resistance' of the other does not do violence to me, does not act negatively; it has a positive structure: ethical." (pp. 155–6, quoting within from Levinas, 1969, *Totality and Infinity*)

He further goes on to depict the approach to the other that is relevant to resistance: "Contrary to Hegel, I do not first feel myself threatened when I confront the other; instead, I realize that I threaten the other and that the other is my fundamental responsibility" (p. 161).

Understood this way, ethical resistance as a component of teacher professionalism is not so much about how teachers are subjected in structures of domination, but how they enact structures of domination over their students, failing to answer their students' pleas (by their very presence) not to be harmed. Called for then is a rather fundamental notion of professional ethics, a fundamental turn to the relation of the self and other that addresses the potential for threat and violence between the self and the other.

Hoy positions Levinas as believing that ethical resistance is a necessary precondition of social resistance. "Why would power be exerted in the name of social emancipation, the Levinasian might well ask, if this exercise of power were not at the same time recognition of the obligation to the powerless?" (p. 182). Hoy makes the further point that while these ethical obligations are fundamental, they are also unenforceable and therefore the province of the ethical. As he says, "Obligations that were enforced would, by virtue of the force behind them, not be freely undertaken and would not be in the realm of the ethical" (p. 185). By implication, no accountability system can enforce this ethicality. It is rather something that an educator decides to acknowledge and take on. (Philosophers craft arguments to persuade others to think about their lives in new ways. It is up to the reader to decide an action as the next step. As in this book, I invite the reader to consider how this active/ethical framework may work for him or her.)

A tentative conclusion

With this formulation, Hoy provides me with exactly the rationale I need to frame educator professionalism, for he lays out the necessity for both social resistance and ethical resistance, with ethical resistance as the necessary precondition. As someone who teaches in a School of Education, I can imagine promoting social resistance through providing teacher education and leadership preparation students with genealogical or quasi-genealogical accounts of high-stakes accountability policy that expose the foreclosed possibilities. Further, I can provide students with experiences of collaboration and communication across difference, which may provide them practice with self-constitution not just within themselves but in communities that provide connection.

Imagining what we may do to promote ethical resistance is a more challenging task, particularly since it is difficult to even get an audience before educators. Philosophy of education has become increasingly marginalized in the preparation of teachers, educational administrators, and other school personnel. The study of ethics is too often a bad fit for what educators face in schools. It may be on one hand geared toward the philosophical traditions, which may be difficult to translate into the power relations of schooling. On the other hand, ethics instruction may be geared more toward expectations and standards of state law or professional associations, which may address minimal expectations for personal conduct. In either case, students may envision a much different sense of obligation than Hoy draws from Levinas. As Hoy advocates, ethical resistance is a fundamental component of resistance, and it is therefore a crucial component in the resistance to normalization wrought by the phenomenon of high-stakes accountability. How might we call ethical resistance into action?

For teacher education students, my best attempt would be to connect to their impulses for wanting to teach, taking advantage of their missionary zeal to develop a sense of appreciation for the power dynamics built into that zeal and helping to question how they are conceptualizing the other in that dynamic. Incorporating this work into field experiences, as Ladson-Billings (2001) demonstrates in her work on culturally relevant pedagogy, would be essential to cultivating ethical resistance as an orientation toward the other. In this way, I have a chance to help them see their work as something like a Foucauldian project of self-constitution, wherein they improve themselves as selves through their interaction with others.

For graduate students already with experience in education, I can more easily tap into their notions that their profession has shortchanged them on enactments of their ethics. For them, the task is similar to my own— Greene's (1988) call to "reawaken the consciousness of possibility" (p. 23). Here actually is where we have our best work to do, because we have in our colleagues who are graduate students in school leadership and other relevant fields bodies willing to imagine a subject position for themselves that fosters ethical resistance not only in themselves, but their colleagues and students. They have come to this point because of the startlingly overreaching exercises of power that make them partners in the domination of students. They largely know that their work has been made unsustainable ethically, and they are eager to see the possibilities that have been foreclosed. Hoy suggests that genealogy and deconstruction are the methods for making this happen. And I suggest that even a little of that—enough to give them a sense of how they might constitute themselves differently as ethical subjects and resistant professionals—will go a long way.

As the interview excerpts that open this chapter suggest, each educator faces his or her own ethical resistance challenges. No ethical framework that purports to follow the care of the self would suggest that all those who follow should end up looking alike. I also do not want to leave readers with the impression that Bryan is the more morally upstanding example or the paradigm example of the care of the self. However, I do think that the situation within which he works is more amenable to the cultivation of professionalism for both teachers and school leaders. The district's attempt to broaden its students' perspective on the world through its global citizenship initiative will undoubtedly continue to play out in interesting ways as parents and students in that district increasingly become positioned in the larger discourse as consumers of educational services. If, as evidence suggests, the teachers' intentions are to help foster students' sense of inter-connection with the rest of the world, the content of that curriculum may come into conflict with the students' own positioning as privileged consumers of a higher-status public education than students not only in other parts of the world, but in school districts adjacent to their own.

I hope for the educators whose words were excerpted here (necessarily with limited context), to draw from their fundamental commitments to their students, to think of how they interact with them as ethical (I have no doubt they would get that) but also capable of exactly the kind of resistance to normalization so desperately needed. I am less sure what I have said so far will complete the picture. Practical next steps follow.

8

The active/ethical professional in practice

In this final chapter, I revisit various examples used throughout the text to show how an active/ethical framework for professional ethics may inform educators' practice and help them to be vigilant against the dangers associated with high-stakes accountability policy. The emphasis in this chapter is on practices and dispositions that can make a difference on a day-to-day basis. As I have mentioned throughout the text, social action is also crucial, and so I have some things to say about that aspect of the active/ethical framework also. I resist the temptation to normalize the educators in these stories. It would violate the spirit of the project to sort and characterize the various educators as models of resistance or acquiescence. My idea is not to tell them what they should do, to diagnose their problems, or to offer pat solutions to those supposed problems (in this group, the educators that I know personally can certainly handle themselves, so I have no illusions here). Instead, the idea is to help us as readers of these stories think differently about what we are reading, so that we might open up possibilities for our own practice.

First I have a caveat: it is not likely to be constructive to implore teachers, school leaders, and other members of school communities to develop and adopt my philosophy of education or any other philosophy of education that ignores the context and pressures of high-stakes accountability policy. I did not set out to argue for a completely different state of affairs in public education. Certainly the best chance for substantive change in the negative effects associated with high-stakes accountability policy would be significant changes to federal educational policy. If we must keep some notion of public school accountability, we would need to define it such that whole communities, including policymakers, share in responsibility for high standards and equity in education (Sirotnik, 2004). At every level is needed dialogue informed by multiple philosophies of education, but of course national policy does not work that way. There is also no reason to believe that a substantive change in national education policy is on the horizon. Instead, I write these recommendations for school districts, schools, individual educators, schools of education, and school collectives (I say more about these later) who have a greater chance of making a difference in educational experiences of children on a day-to-day basis. The guiding question for this chapter is: what can an active/ethical professional do?

Jill Bartoni's story

I begin with a specific and practical answer from Jill Bartoni, whose story opens the book. Jill has thought quite a bit about how high-stakes accountability policy leads to normalizing behaviors in schools, including those with which she feels complicit. A long while ago she developed a way to bring her concerns into the high school language arts curriculum:

> I have been doing this—this has been my way of trying to assuage some of my guilt about being complicit in these things. I start the year with an essay by [Sydney J.] Harris about what a true education should do. In that essay, Harris talks about—it's an old piece—but he talks about students being sausage casings. And the way that education has always been constructed and often enacted is that teachers stuffed them. And they laugh at that—"Do you want to be a sausage casing?"—and I start there and I talk about that, and I try to get them to think about meaningful learning experiences they have had and to write about that. And then I bring in early on Adrienne Rich's notion of owning your own education. And I tell them, "In this class, that is what you're going to have to do, and some of you are going to be very upset about this." And early on they are like, "Oh wow, we have this teacher who jumps around the room and wow," but when I actually start to plan that out in the day-to-day practice as it informs my pedagogy—because I do believe as [Parker] Palmer says, "We teach who we are"—it's hard. It's hard for them.

Question our education

Jill has told us that, over time, even her strongest students seem to have become focused more on performing than on learning. They seek good grades more so than the knowledge and experience that come from learning. So one of the primary suggestions from Jill is having students question their own education. Bryan Tennyson says almost the same thing in the excerpt from his interview in Chapter 7 when he says that the hardest part of high school is getting students to take ownership of their own learning.

The hope is that in questioning their education, students will be moved to be more intentional and choose experiences that help them with the project of their lives—the care of the self as a project of continual self-constitution. As Noddings (2007) helps us to see, we can use self-questioning to consider alternatives to the ways in which schooling seems to be moving students toward greater homogeneity. Those who help students question their educations can be ready with nonnormalized perspectives on alternatives to the drumbeat that to be successful, all high school graduates must be prepared for college. Interrupting that discourse with examples of alternative routes can provide students with ways to imagine themselves enacting alternatives. When I have administrators from career and technical education centers in my classes, by their testimony of experiences in class discussions, they interrupt dominant notions of secondary school success and the tendency to construct career and technical education as a deviant trajectory.

Debbie Bendick's story

In Debbie Bendick's story, she found herself captivated by her colleague's ability to craft deep, meaningful relationships with his faculty, and she suspected that these relationships were part of the secret to his success in student achievement in his school. Once Debbie disentangled Jess' community building efforts and the test score performance of his students, she ended up with an enhanced appreciation for the dynamics of the relational ethics upon which Jess created his school community.

A language of relation

Through her dissertation, Debbie was able to create for herself a language of relation to describe what she valued about her colleague's school. We can all take a lesson from Debbie's experience. In whatever normalizing policy contexts educators find themselves, it may help them to return continually to the primary relation of the teacher and student (Biesta, 2004). Because so much of high-stakes accountability policy shifts the primary relation to be the one between the state and the school, the pedagogical relation should be protected and nurtured, keeping it at the center of educational decision making. Like Debbie, other educators need a language of relation that would enable them to build educational experiences from that starting point. They can develop a language of relation from Foucault's care of the self or any number of the other educational theories from Chapter 3 that place ethics as primary. One of the features of a language of relation that we miss relates to the location of her story in a largely affluent suburban community. A school district such as Debbie's, which is well-positioned for accountability, is not the only place where the pedagogical relation can be protected and cultivated.

Make relations problematic

As those who work with educators, we could do a better job of helping each other understand at least three things about relations. These features need attention regardless of the ethical theory that we adopt, although using an ethical theory such as Foucault's in tandem may help us make better use of any other chosen ethical theory. The three concerns about relations are as follows: (a) there is power exercised in relations that is inescapable; (b) the teacher/student relation is a particular kind of site for power, characterized by inherently unequal power relations and nonreciprocal responsibility; and (c) there is an important distinction between accountability and responsibility, the rupture of which can systematically destroy the freedom-forming potential of that relation.

What would it mean to center the relation may be found in the work of Freire (2000/1970), who advocates problem-posing education as an alternative to the more conventional banking education. Similarly to Noddings' (1984) ethic of caring, the pedagogical relation is primary, and the motivation for education is *what is important to the student*. But what if we do not know? By making relations problematic, we question the taken-for-granted nature of our relations and work to be more intentional. An educator may ask himself: What do I see as my responsibility to this student? What limits do I impose upon that relation? What conditions do I seem to impose upon the student before I am willing to accept responsibility? What am I assuming I know about this student that is influencing what I believe to be our relationship and my responsibility? These are all important questions to ask of ourselves as educators so that we might improve the quality of our relations. As educators, we may filter our actions through the concept of the relation, depending on our answers to these questions.

Policy makers can manipulate educators into succumbing to accountability pressures because of the close tie to responsibility. Educators can use the language of responsibility to talk about their relations with children differently and encourage each other to choose actions that make them responsible for students, which is more important than how someone else defines them to be accountable for students. Doing so requires multiple tactics, the most obvious being exposure to the concepts, but perhaps not so obvious, centering the relational aspect of teaching in practice, preparation, and evaluation. Rhetoric is after all quite powerful, and one way to resist is to capture some rhetoric to make a resistant idea sound clearer to those who would be inclined to listen or to shake up those not inclined to listen.

Sid Davidson's story

At the end of Sid's story, I posed a series of questions that I said a post-structural ethics would do well to answer. I return to those now, drawing from the whole of my argument in the text for thinking about Sid's situation differently.

- *How might Sid help his teachers more effectively see how they have the opportunity to rethink their reluctance to resist the chanting curriculum? How might Sid come to understand what is behind teachers' trepidation to follow their better judgment? If part of the teachers' trepidation is emotional, how can they draw on ethics that may emotionally support them acting on their better judgment?*

In Sid's story, the teachers did not seem convinced that they could close the door and avoid teaching the chanted curriculum. The example calls to mind Zembylas' (2003) story of how Catherine reconstituted herself emotionally as a successful teacher by attending to the affective responses that students had to her work with them. Knowing more about the teachers' reluctance to resist would go a long way toward understanding how power relations are working on them and suppressing their resistance. The trope in Zembylas' example is reconstitution—taking control over the meanings one makes from various influences: what the newspaper says about their school, the sense they make of differential test scores, and perhaps most importantly, the ways in which they assess their own performance as a teacher. In a sense, Sid's story presents stark choices: to chant or not to chant. Perhaps more important is what else they do with the chanting (or without it with another method), how and why they do it, and how they figure out how well they are teaching and what students are getting out of the experience. Overall, how does it contribute to an education relation that is expansive for both teacher and student? A mentor may help teachers in similar situations to develop alternative means to assess their teaching practices, so that not only would they have justifications for their own practices, but they might also have alternative means for questioning them and improving them.

- *How might the curriculum director question how the district's own practices (particularly the ones the district is freely implementing because it is focused on compliance) work against its better judgment about what is worthwhile for students to do and learn? How might district leadership create conditions that encourage school leaders and teachers to innovate freely and avoid the dangers associated with the well-documented effects of high-stakes accountability policy, especially in school districts like this one that does not meet all of its accountability targets?*

It does not pay to demonize the curriculum director, who in Sid's style of conversation may come across as an unsympathetic figure. Attributing the best motives to the man in the context of the situation, we could imagine that he is at the very least exasperated with the position that he is in and perhaps lacks alternatives. It does seem that seeking alternatives is at least possible in this situation. It seems that the district has capacity that it is underutilizing—the teachers believe they are more skilled than the chanting curriculum makes them out to be—so one way to rethink the situation is to take stock of the capacity in the district and build intentionally from there. Although there are no guarantees that building from strengths will lead to the same kind of compliance that test preparation does, it does seem that rethinking responsibility for the curriculum beyond a single decision maker may lead to more sustainable gains in capacity.

- *How might Sid help his teachers rethink the role that the six children play in the philosophy of education of the school? How might they use the example of these children to reframe their notion of responsibility?*

It seems that we have in this example a very strong example of the combined dangers of normalization and the state/school relation taking primacy. We have the opportunity for educators to create something different through dialogue among Sid and his teachers. What if we were to reposition the education of these six children (the six who Sid says seem to show up in all the school's subgroups that are at most risk of not testing well and therefore keeping the school from making AYP) as the most important mission of the school? What would the school look like if we were to reorganize the school in order to make the quality of these six children's education the best it could be? (Of course we would have to define what that would be in dialogue, which would be a vital process just by itself.)

To go a bit further and to risk a more volatile conversation, what if we were to bring to the surface the lack of expressed racism toward these students that Sid mentions? And what if we were to consider this line of thinking—since no one seems to harbor racist attitudes toward these students, we will start from the assumption that no one does. What if we entertained the possibility that racism still might be an important factor in why the same six children across these subgroups are all male and all African American? Such a discussion, while potentially volatile, might help not only rethink education for these children but also rethink how racism operates in tandem with normalization, and give educators an appreciation of how difficult it is to counter racism, partly because it is so difficult for people to separate racism from racists (the dialogue may help educators to define racism as an exercise of power, as opposed to a trait of an individual). Such a rethinking may allow stronger ownership of these children, become explicitly (or strategically) proud of them, forestalling blaming them in the future, or forestalling resentment if more children in the subgroups begin to enroll in the school. Such an exercise would work to resist the ways in which accountability policy invites stigmatizing subgroups, ironically discouraging educators from wanting to take responsibility for their education.

Other ethical traditions

Next, although I do think that post-structural ethics helps us to see the significance of the pedagogical relation in our current context, I do not insist that post-structural ethics are the only models (or even necessarily the best models) for planning moral action in pedagogical relations. Any number of ethical frames may be appropriate for moral action. Moral frames and theories are often tied to deeply personal views, including deeply held spiritual beliefs. In teaching about professional ethics, I do prefer compelling people with the significance of relation first, however, because of the primary importance of the pedagogical relation, so that they can immediately see the day-to-day relevance of ethical theory, then tap into whatever theories speak to their moral intuitions most resoundingly. Chapter 3 includes examples of authors who speak to multiple educators' moral intuitions. These are all workable ways to ground the pedagogical relation, and these can be effective for resistance to the dangers of high-stakes accountability policy as long as educators can couple their ethical theory with a sophisticated understanding of power relations.

The story of the A+ Schools Network

The stories of the A+ Schools in North Carolina and Oklahoma opened the chapter on responsibility, because of the ways in which these schools had an opportunity to use arts integration as an educational idea around which to build their educational philosophies, which in turn enabled them to take better responsibility for their students' educational experiences. There are some additional features to the network that I would like to highlight in this chapter, because they offer approaches that other schools and groups of schools may wish to consider, whether or not the arts are involved.

Professional collectives

In both states that developed A+ Networks, the framers of the reform found unexpected value in the networking aspect of the schools that came together to learn about and implement the A+ essentials. The reformers were initially focused on making a difference in as many schools as possible, but something more emerged. The first evidence of this emergence came during the first year in North Carolina among the principals (Noblit et al., 2009). Principals realized that they were having many of the same challenges in their practice, and they were able to help each other think about how arts integration could help them with those challenges. It also reinforced to them and to the organizers of the program the importance of the process of whole-school reform, encouraging from that point onward a systems approach to professional development. The research team also came to realize the value to schools of continual engagement in the process. We came to realize that looking for the schools to become models of arts integration missed the value of the reform. Being involved in A+ meant a commitment to continual learning on the part of teachers and school leaders, and schools were to come together to support each other in that continual learning. In that sense, the schools began to act as professional communities and take responsibility for their own practice.

This observation points out the benefit of professional collectives for resistance. In Western Pennsylvania, we have a number of collectives that bring educators together to share ideas and build capacity. These collectives can be quite powerful and work against the competitive nature of high-stakes accountability. The Forum for Western Pennsylvania School Superintendents is an example of one such collective which meets semiannually around issues of concern to superintendents. Sharing within the collective and professional development from specialists outside the collective has for the Forum's entire existence been focused on how superintendents can be more effective advocates for children in the region.

Sam Galloway's story

Sam's story of multiple power relations in operation in response to and because of high-stakes accountability policy provides ideas that run the gamut for rethinking how schools are affected.

Responding to questionable decisions

One of the most interesting things about Sam's experience is his confidence in enacting his philosophy of education while under the conditions of NCLB. Sam implies elsewhere in his interview that he found it difficult under a previous superintendent to obtain resources for the elementary and middle schools, when resources for the district's high school seemed to be the top priority. Sam was in a position to respond to questionable decisions made above him. In his current situation, he works to help teachers avoid making questionable decisions below him. One can imagine someone in a similar situation facing cases when questionable decisions further are being made beside him—such as another principal in the district, or a colleague in a competing, neighboring district. Sid's story repeats examples of incidents like these.

Educators need help with ways to respond when those above, below, or beside them in the educational hierarchy make questionable decisions. So many of the normalizing power relations in education are occurring, according to the literature, not even from NCLB itself, but from state and district policies put in place to comply with NCLB. The normalizing decisions—and I am not just speaking of cheating—are proliferating. Educators need ways to question the reasons for those decisions, speaking from positions of strength and confidence that, for instance, the default philosophy of education is indefensible. I would propose a rule that raising test scores cannot by itself be a legitimate reason for any educational decision; a second reason must be provided, and it must be a substantive reason grounded in a philosophy of education (no second reason is acceptable that can be logically reduced to raising test scores).

Engage high standards

If schools can indeed agree that standards-based reform fits with their philosophies of education, then the most appropriate way to deal with high-stakes accountability is to engage not with the tests but with the high standards. This involves connecting themselves with the curriculum that the district or state is expecting them to study. As it happened in the A+ Schools, those participating in the program had been encouraged already to focus on the state curriculum—a laundry list curriculum that was nevertheless adaptable to two-way arts integration and thematic integration—and to teach its subject matter in its entirety. These schools needed to become familiar with the entire scope and sequence of the state curriculum so that they could more effectively integrate the arts across the curriculum; those who did so effectively were also effective in warding off the default philosophy encouraged by the high-stakes accountability program (Noblit et al., 2009).

The more recent invention of curriculum "anchors" serves only to encourage schools to teach to the test in a more sophisticated manner. Schools that, again, are inclined to focus on the state curriculum may trump the standards by organizing themselves around higher-order concepts and more enriched engagements than the standards. This alternative resists the weakness of laundry-list standards that encourage mile-wide, inch-deep "coverage" of tested material. Excessive focus on knowledge works against the cultivation of selves capable of thinking and exploring possibilities. Teachers at Olympus High School are doing that, and there is no reason that teachers elsewhere could not do the same thing.

Iris Lorenzo's story

We get the impression from Iris' interview that she goes about her work rather independently and without much help or interference from her peers or her supervisors, who occasionally create some distracting noise around her in the form of threats on her performance, which she apparently attempts subtly to pass on to her students, albeit more gently. Even if this impression is distorted by the limited evidence of the interview, there are several important things to learn from Iris' story about engaging in professional practices with integrity and some resistance.

Treat students as ends

Iris has a handle on responsibility, perhaps born out of her background in special education. She does not see herself as responsible for a classroom but for each individual student. It is difficult to improve upon that philosophy, and unfortunately the condition of NCLB that all subgroups demonstrate proficiency by 2014 has made this definition of responsibility noncompliant. It also seems to turn other children's parents against children in subgroups (Hamilton et al., 2007). A responsibility discourse may be brought to bear to call out such people and name the dangers associated with such attitudes.

Plan substantively rational goals

In contrast to the rampant instrumentality that high-stakes accountability policy encourages, Iris is only the slightest bit fretful that she spent two weeks on a special activity in which her students imagined themselves as sports reporters and collected statistics that helped them learn statistical concepts such as mean, median, and mode. Iris tells us that she is glad that she did it, even though it put her behind on the district's pacing guide and meant that there was that much less material that she was able to cover before testing. With this activity, Iris planned an activity that was substantively rational. She encouraged students to imagine themselves in a future role, creating open-ended possibilities for them to create meaning about the concepts under study.

Engage parents

Following Iris' lead, relations with parents are especially significant as relations between schools and families become economic consumer relations (Biesta, 2004). Iris actively works against the easier route by engaging parents as often as possible. It is incumbent upon educators to have tools to form other kinds of relations. There are tensions in my graduate courses when practicing educators speak variously about "supportive parents," "overbearing parents," and "parents who don't care"; at times I did it myself (and might still if I dealt with my students' parents). Quite often I hear pathologizing about parents, their interests, and their dispositions toward their children. Iris models a less antagonistic stance toward parents. I often hear stories that suggest that educators wish to manage the concerns of parents or manipulate them to support their agendas as educator. More needs to be done to foster the relationships of respect and mutual responsibility that may contribute to ethical self-formation.

Stories from Carol Trent, Carl Castillo, and Bryan Tennyson

The three juxtaposed stories of Carol, Carl, and Bryan provide multiple views on what resistance looks like or could look like within the active/ethical framework. Important across all three stories is realizing that conditions for resistance are contingent: a change of leadership, for instance, can make the grounds for resistance change overnight.

Turn resistance into something active

My rationale for bringing these three stories together was to show subtle resistance and overt resistance. There is truly some form of resistance for everyone, and while I believe that resistance to normalization should be the crucial goal for the active/ethical framework, I know that resistance carries a negative connotation for many educators, who are predominantly, like me, the ones who liked school, paid attention, and caused little trouble for their teachers (although some of the most interesting teachers I know are the ones who apparently were hellions as students). I would like educators to expand their comfort with the central importance of resistance and what can count as resistance. It struck me still several years ago when I first read an interview transcript in which a teacher talked about surreptitiously teaching social studies to her students, because it had been crowded out of the curriculum by her superiors' insistence on test preparation. How dangerous things had become, I thought, when teaching social studies is resistance, and this was not even the kind of ideological social studies that upset Lynne Cheney so much! So many principled, professional stances are in fact resistant to the dangers of high-stakes accountability policy, and it is important for educators to appreciate that, even if they might prefer to call it active/ethical.

Take the principled risk

Spaces for engaging in risk are curtailed in the context of high-stakes accountability. In his work, Pignatelli (2002) addresses the importance of risk for any Foucauldian resistance to high-stakes accountability. The willingness to risk is a natural enemy to oppressive discursive practices and to acquiescence to normalization. Moments when risks need to be taken may be fleeting, and I suspect that many of the most important ones may be outside the classroom—on teacher work days, at meetings in the school district, and during interviews with local media. These are examples of opportunities that Pignatelli refers to as opportunities for speaking truth to power, but speaking out need not be as heroic as that sounds.

Taking a risk against normalization also need not be thought of solely as "risking one's job," as some have done (Weaver, 2003). We may be tempted to think about risk first in terms of placing oneself at risk—speaking out against subjugating practices, for example, and risking one's job. The link between risk and resistance need not be so individualistic. Freire (2005/1997) argues that teachers need to act collectively and build support from parents and students for their professional judgment.

Welch (2000) speaks of risk as an essential countercultural strategy for working against oppressive conditions. Risk works against the cultural preference for control, the cultural need (at least in the United States) for complete answers to problems, regardless of how complicated they are. Applied to education, taking a risk may be as simple as trusting a student or a colleague, or experimenting with something new that is not scientifically proven to maximize test score gains, or spending time on something interesting that is not aligned with a standard or a test. An ethical decision is often a risk, but it is also for Foucault an exercise of power that opens up possibilities of new institutional practices and social arrangements.

Difference

The experience of difference, so crucial to Foucauldian self-formation, is also a promising, meaningful approach for educators. Through varied experiences of difference, it is surmised, educators are more likely to make themselves open to possibilities. This is crucial if we expect educators and administrators to imagine alternatives to the oppressive practices associated with high-stakes accountability. As has been noted throughout the literature, some of the most deleterious effects of high-stakes accountability have resulted from educators changing their structures and practices in order for their students and schools merely to look better in accountability schemes. In some cases, educators may feel they have no choice.

What is often underappreciated, in relation to experiences such as this, is the long-term educative potential of disruptive educational experiences.

As Alice McIntyre (1997) demonstrates, students given a series of unsettling experiences designed to get them to challenge the privilege associated with their own whiteness seemed to "not get it" during the semester she worked with them. Yet for several students, even their next semester teacher education experiences were transformed by their experiences. We know little about the long-term effects of experiences of difference, since little research is conducted about the ongoing constitution of the self. Memoirs tell a different story (e.g., Rothenberg, 2000), giving a strong sense that self-constitution proceeds at varied paces, defies assessment in any traditional assessment, and yet is as important as any educational outcome.

Final thoughts

More needs to be done to counter the dangers of high-stakes accountability policy. The jobs of educators have become more difficult, and the need for robust notions of professionalism is more necessary than ever. Educators have much to do to name the disciplinary apparatus associated with high-stakes accountability, identify its genealogical ancestors and contemporary contradictions, and articulate alternatives. Philosophers of education have their tasks alongside educators, including exposing the philosophical basis for the misuse of the technology of the examination, articulating alternative philosophies of education, developing rationales for how certain practices have been illegitimately foreclosed, providing theoretical support for colleagues whose research into innovative practices has been sidetracked by the ascendancy of the standardized test, and analyzing rhetoric surrounding accountability. My hope is for more collaboration between educators and philosophers of education.

In such a climate of ethical complications, schools of education have multiple crucial roles for preparing educators and administrators that may be more actively ethical and resistant to the dangers of high-stakes accountability policy. High-stakes accountability programs have led to so much normalizing educational practice that an increasingly significant concern for social foundations faculty teaching in education graduate programs has become educating for resistance. My contention throughout this book is that resistance should be grounded in a professionalism that incorporates a robust philosophy of education and sense of professional ethics.

At the same time, I have recently become more convinced that ethical rigidity is also quite dangerous. Taking solely a moral orientation toward pedagogical relations is also problematic. While this may seem counterintuitive, the drive to serve is a powerful motivator for reforming schools, but the crusading zeal often evident in Teach for America and the autocratic arrogance of powerful elite school reformers such as Michelle

Rhee are as much hubris as moral orientation toward schooling. The phrase "ethical hubris" occurred to me while preparing remarks about the documentary *Waiting for Superman,* which I found unexpectedly pedestrian in its summary of the social foundations of education and then remarkably dense for its lack of attention to educational ideas. Providing contradictory evidence for its championing of charter schools, the film made a hero out of Michelle Rhee and a villain out of Randi Weingarten, whose union was vilified with no more evidence than the opinions of the film's heroes (as Ravitch [2010] shows, union states tend to have higher average achievement and although not entirely blameless are merely the latest scapegoats). I was left to conclude that the filmmakers overdid their moral certainty. Post-structural ethics teaches that no one has provenance over what is ethically defensible. Innocent intention is a poor excuse for bad manners. The problem is that the pedagogical relation is not innocent, teachers need to be aware of their power, and they need to attend actively to *things that they can do.* It calls to mind a point quoted earlier in this book that commitment alone is a disservice to students if a teacher is not capable (paraphrase of Oakes et al., 2004, p. 89). This is an apt critique of the underlying logic of rewards and sanctions, because forcing schools without appropriate capacity to work harder not only wears these people out but drains them of their moral agency.

To undercut my own ethical hubris, I return to the first argument I made about high-stakes accountability policy many years ago—above all, despite pressures from high-stakes accountability and outsized testing programs, it is crucial that educators and school communities remain engaged in dialogue about the value and purposes of education that provide the goals for public education. Teachers, schools, and districts can develop rich philosophies of education that are based not only on reflections on practice but the careful consideration of alternative visions. And finally, educators who risk and embrace difference put themselves in the position of caring for themselves and establish more promising conditions for students to care for themselves. In doing so, we can resist normalization and grow in our active/ethical professionalism.

APPENDIX
Studies of accountability and school reform

Stories presented at the beginning of Chapters 1 through 7 come from university-based research studies in which I have participated during the period 1995–2011 as a doctoral student and faculty member. The book is not a report of these research studies or even a synthesis of what my collaborators and I learned during the projects. The philosophical analysis takes center stage in the book, so that I have ample space to work through the various arguments and subarguments that go into the active/ethical framework. I have written and cowritten some work from these research studies, and several others likewise have addressed this topic in their work. Several University of Pittsburgh doctoral students have collected, analyzed, and written from this data, and we have plans to do more of that in the future. The studies helped shape my thinking about how high-stakes accountability policy has come to influence educational practice. Engaging stories from these studies over the course of writing this book has further pushed my thinking, and I hope the stories chosen for the book provide the reader with greater clarity.

In this brief appendix, I describe the methodology behind the studies to provide additional context and to explain how I have situated myself during this time as both a qualitative researcher and philosopher of education. As noted, more expansive details about the two A+ Schools research projects are also published elsewhere.

Research and evaluation of the North Carolina A+ Schools Program (1995–9)

As a doctoral student, I was funded for four years of study as part of a mixed-methods research and evaluation team based at the University of North Carolina at Chapel Hill and funded by the Thomas S. Kenan Institute for the Arts. As I explain at the opening of Chapter 4, the North Carolina (N.C.) A+ Schools Program is an arts-integration, whole-school reform initiative that has achieved remarkable sustainability over the 16 years of its existence. Led by George Noblit, Dick Corbett, and Bruce Wilson, the research team studied 27 A+ schools: two pilot schools that began A+ prior to the Kenan Institute's involvement and 25 schools that began implementing the program together in 1995. One school discontinued its involvement for funding reasons at the end of the first year. We collected data at schools from 1995 to 1999, with an additional year for report preparation. For the first four years, I was one of up to ten doctoral students funded by the project at any one time.

As doctoral student researchers, we collected data from the 27 schools in the form of (a) surveys of principals, parents, students, and teachers; (b) test scores; and (c) qualitative data in the form of participant-observation of classrooms, planning meetings, and performances; focus groups with teachers and students; individual interviews with teachers, administrators, community partners, and parents; and various documents, including planning materials, newsletters, meeting minutes, and school improvement plans (Nelson, 2001). I collected portions of data at 16 schools, and I conducted in-depth case studies of a rural school, Sandy Fork Elementary, and an urban school, Creekside Elementary. For two years, I visited Sandy Fork and Creekside about two days a month during the academic year, and during the last year of the study, I visited less frequently to receive updates on the schools' progress. Over my time at the schools, I interviewed virtually every teacher in the school at least once using a semistructured interview protocol at first, and then eventually conducted follow-up interviews to round out our team's emerging themes. During the school year, the research team met weekly to generate themes across schools and to inform each others' case study analyses. Cindy Gerstl-Pepin and I wrote an article about the method we called collaborative team ethnography (Gerstl-Pepin & Gunzenhauser, 2002).

Final reports were published in 2001. A comprehensive book summarizes the results of the study and a follow-up study several years later (Noblit, et al., 2009). The N.C. A+ Schools Network is still in operation under the direction of the N.C. Arts Council. A thorough website (aplus-schools.ncdcr. gov) details the history and evolution of the program.

Research and evaluation of the Oklahoma A+ Schools (2002–7)

In one of life's coincidences, I was working at Oklahoma State University when the Kirkpatrick Foundation and the DaVinci Institute in Oklahoma City collaborated with the N.C. A+ Schools Network to start the Oklahoma A+ Schools, another well-sustaining whole-school reform network that has experienced steady growth and expansion. For two years, I was coprincipal investigator with Nancy Barry, Michael Raiber, and Diane Montgomery on a research and evaluation study that Nancy and Michael continued and expanded after I relocated to the University of Pittsburgh in 2004. They completed five years of data collection and published their reports in January 2010 (including Raiber et al. [2010]).

In the first two years of the study, we initially based our research design on the N.C. research and then added data collection instruments to serve the research questions of the network's directors. Nancy and Michael eventually expanded the methodology quite extensively, with the final reports making use of data from 38 schools and child development centers in the form of (a) four survey instruments: a yearly student survey, two yearly teacher surveys, and a survey for the professional development specialists; (b) extensive qualitative data in the form of classroom observations, professional development session observations, photographs of activities and student products, artifacts supplied by schools, and interviews with teachers, school leaders, parents, and community partners; and (c) assessment and accountability data (Hendrickson, 2010). The team conducted participant observation studies at A+ summer institutes and visited each school periodically for classroom observations and teacher and school leader interviews. I personally collected survey, observational and interview data at several summer institutes and workshop sessions, planning meetings, and at four of the schools. The Oklahoma A+ Schools are under the direction of Jean Hendrickson. The Schools' website (aplusok.org) contains the various research reports and extensive information about the schools.

High-stakes testing and philosophies of education (2003–present) and innovation in the accountability era (2009–present)

In 2003, Judie Mathers and I started a joint research project at Oklahoma State University to capture the experiences of teachers and administrators in Oklahoma public schools as they were just beginning to experience standards-based reform and high-stakes accountability for the first time. We first surveyed Oklahoma teachers and principals about their beliefs about accountability, responsibility, rewards, and sanctions (Mathers, 2004). We then formed a research team with a group of graduate students to conduct semistructured interviews with a cross-section of teachers throughout the state in elementary, middle, and high schools. The interview protocol focused on educators' beliefs about the meaning and value of education, asking in several different ways what educators believe their philosophies of education to be, how day-to-day practice enables them and disables them from enacting their philosophies, and for educators who are unable to enact their philosophies of education, what opportunities they see to resist. When I relocated to the University of Pittsburgh in Summer 2004, Judie continued with the study and a new team. The project eventually produced about 20 in-depth interviews. Doctoral students, Judie, and I generated conference papers from the data.

In 2006, I collaborated with Andrea Hyde, then a doctoral student, to recreate the interview study in Pennsylvania. After pausing our collaboration while Andrea worked independently on her dissertation on the topic (Hyde, 2007), the data collection recommenced, and through various combinations of doctoral students over the years, that study is ongoing, with a database of about 40 in-depth interviews and growing as new students come into the project with new interests in the philosophical questions raised in the data and new samples of Pennsylvania educators. We have used the original Oklahoma interview protocol adapted for the Pennsylvania context and with follow-up interviews tailored to the specific subthemes generated in the data. Various students and I have written conference papers from the data, and the team is currently working on articles for publication.

In 2009, the research team developed an offshoot project, called *Innovation in the Accountability Era,* to conduct case studies of schools and districts attempting to innovate while under pressure of external accountability. The case study methodology is designed to complement the variation of experiences that have emerged from individual interviews with context-based studies of processes within schools. In collaboration with me and Pitt faculty colleague John Myers, the first of these case studies is underway by doctoral student Marzia Cozzolino and alumna Jillian Bichsel, who are studying the implementation of a global citizenship program in a high school that is well-positioned for external accountability. The study has taken on the form of an ethnographic case study, with participant-observation and semi-structured interviews the primary methods of data collection. This project has produced conference papers about the innovative idea itself and data on the enactment of professionalism in a well-positioned district.

REFERENCES

107th Congress (2002). *The Elementary and Secondary Education Act. The No Child Left Behind Act of 2001.* Washington, DC: 107th Congress. Retrieved from http://www.ed.gov/legislation/ESEA02/pg1.html

American Evaluation Association (2002). American Evaluation Association position statement on high-stakes testing in PreK-12 education. Retrieved from http://www.eval.org/hst3.htm

Amrein-Beardsley, Audrey, David C. Berliner, & Sharon Rideau (2010). Cheating in the first, second, and third degree: Educators' responses to high-stakes testing. *Educational Policy Analysis Archives,* 18(14). Retrieved from http://epaa.asu.edu/ojs/article/view/714

Anderson, Gary (2009). *Advocacy leadership: Toward a post-reform agenda in education.* New York: Routledge.

Aristotle (1962). *Nicomachean ethics* (Martin Ostwald, trans.). Englewood Cliffs, NJ: Prentice-Hall. (Original work published c. 4th Century BC.)

Baker Paula B. & Lee W. Digiovanni (2005). Narratives on culturally relevant pedagogy: Personal responses to the standardized curriculum. *Current Issues in Education,* 8(22). Retrieved from http://cie.ed.asu.edu/volume8/number22/.

Barth, Roland S. (2001). *Learning by heart.* San Francisco: Jossey-Bass.

Beck, Lynn (1994). *Reclaiming educational administration as a caring profession.* New York: Teachers College Press.

Bendick, Debra M. (2003). *A case study on the role of principal/teacher relationships in building school capacity.* (Unpublished doctoral dissertation. Stillwater, OK: Oklahoma State University.)

Biesta, Gert J. J. (1998). Pedagogy without humanism: Foucault and the subject of education. *Interchange,* 29(1), 1–16.

—(2004). Education, accountability, and the ethical demand: Can the democratic potential of accountability be regained? *Educational Theory,* 54(3), 233–50.

—(2006). *Beyond learning: Democratic education for a human future.* Boulder, CO: Paradigm Publishers.

Blacker, David (1998). Intellectuals at work and in power: Toward a Foucauldian research ethic, in Thomas Popkewitz & Marie Brennan (eds), *Foucault's challenge: Discourse, knowledge, and power in education.* New York: Teachers College Press, pp. 348–67.

—(2003). More than test scores: A liberal contextualist picture of educational accountability. *Educational Theory,* 53(1), 1–18.

Blake, Nigel, Paul Smeyers, Richard Smith, & Paul Standish (1998). *Thinking again: Education after postmodernism.* Westport, CT: Bergin & Garvey.

Boyles, Deron (ed.) (2005). *Schools or markets? Commercialism, privatization, and school-business partnerships*. Mahwah, NJ: Lawrence Erlbaum Associates.

Buber, Martin (1958). *The I and thou* (2nd edn) (Ronald G. Smith, trans.). New York: Charles Scribner's Sons. (Original work published 1923.)

Carnoy, Martin, Richard Elmore, & Leslie S. Siskin (eds) (2003). *The new accountability: High schools and high-stakes testing*. New York: Routledge Falmer.

Cozzolino, Marzia & Jillian Bichsel (2010, November). *Innovation in the accountability era: A case study of a high school*. Paper presented at the annual meeting of the American Educational Studies Association. Denver, CO.

Crotty, Michael (1998). *The foundations of social research: Meaning and perspective in the research process*. London: Sage.

Cuban, Larry (2004). Looking through the rearview mirror at school accountability, in Kenneth A. Sirotnik (ed.), *Holding accountability accountable: What ought to matter in public education*. New York: Teachers College Press, pp. 18–34.

Davies, Bronwyn (2000). *A body of writing*. Walnut Creek, CA: AltaMira Press.

Dewey, John (1966). *Democracy and education*. New York: The Free Press. (Original work published 1916, renewed 1944.)

—(1997). *Experience and education*. New York: Touchstone. (Original work published 1938.)

Dietrich, Joseph J. (2010). *The effect of NCLB on state board and local school board relations: A Pennsylvania example*. (Unpublished doctoral dissertation. Pittsburgh, PA: University of Pittsburgh.)

Dillon, Sam (2011, June 24). Republican challenges administration on plans to override education law. *The New York Times*, A12.

Eisenhart, Margaret & Robert L. DeHaan (2005). Doctoral preparation of scientifically based education researchers. *Educational Researcher*, 34(4), 3–13.

Eisner, Elliot W. (2001). What does it mean to say a school is doing well? *Phi Delta Kappan*, 82(5), 367–72.

—(2002). The kind of schools we need. *Phi Delta Kappan*, 83(8), 576–83.

Ellsworth, Elizabeth (1989). Why doesn't this feel empowering? Working through the repressive myths of critical pedagogy. *Harvard Educational Review*, 59(3), 297–324.

—(1997). *Teaching positions: Difference, pedagogy, and the power of address*. New York: Teachers College Press.

Elmore, Richard F. & Susan H. Fuhrman (2001). Holding schools accountable: Is it working? *Phi Delta Kappan*, 83(1), 67–72.

Erevelles, Nirmala (2002). Voices of silence: Foucault, disability, and the question of self-determination. *Studies in Philosophy and Education*, 21(1), 17–35.

Fendler, Lynn (2004). Praxis and agency in Foucault's historiography. *Studies in Philosophy and Education*, 23(5–6), 445–66.

Feuer, Michael J., Lisa Towne, & Richard J. Shavelson (2002). Scientific culture and educational research. *Educational Researcher*, 31(8), 4–14.

Fine, Michelle (2010). Prologue, in Robert Lake (ed.), *Dear Maxine: Letters from the unfinished conversation with Maxine Greene*. New York: Teachers College Press, pp. xvii–xix.

Finn, Chester (2010, March 3). School's out. *Forbes.com*. Retrieved from http://www.forbes.com/2010/03/02/diane-ravitch-education-schools-opinions-book-reviews-chester-e-finn-jr.html

Fletcher, Scott (2000). *Education and emancipation: Theory and practice in a new constellation*. New York: Teachers College Press.

Ford, Maureen (2003). Unveiling technologies of power in classroom organization practice. *Educational Foundations*, 17(2), 5–27.

Foucault, Michel (1985). *The use of pleasure: The history of sexuality*, Vol. 2 (Robert Hurley, trans.). New York: Vintage Books. (Original work published 1984.)

—(1986). *The care of the self: The history of sexuality*, Vol. 3, reissue edn (Robert Hurley, trans.). New York: Vintage Books. (Original work published 1984)

—(1990). *The history of sexuality, Volume 1: An introduction*, reissue edn (Robert Hurley, trans.). New York: Vintage Books. (Original work published 1976.)

—(1995). *Discipline and punish: The birth of the prison*, 2nd edn (Alan Sheridan, trans.). New York: Vintage Books. (Original work published 1975.)

—(2005). *The hermeneutics of the subject: Lectures at the Collège de France, 1981–82* (Graham Burchell, trans.). New York: Picador. (Original work published 2001.)

Frankena, William K. (1973). *Ethics*, 2nd edn. Englewood Cliffs, NJ: Prentice-Hall.

Franzosa, Susan (1992). Authorizing the educated self: Educational autobiography and resistance, *Educational Theory*, 42(4), 395–412.

Freire, Paulo (2000). *Pedagogy of the oppressed* (Myra B. Ramos, trans.). New York: Continuum. (Original work published 1970.)

—(2005). *Teachers as cultural workers: Letters to those who dare teach*, expanded edn (Donaldo Macedo, Dale Koike, & Alexandre Oliveira, trans.) Boulder, CO: Westview Press. (Original work published 1997.)

Fullan, Michael (2003). *The moral imperative of school leadership*. Thousand Oaks, CA: Corwin Press.

Garrison, James W. (1996). A Deweyan theory of democratic listening. *Educational Theory*, 46(4), 429–51.

—(1998). Foucault, Dewey, and self-creation. *Educational Philosophy and Theory*, 30(2), 111–34.

Gerstl-Pepin, Cynthia I., & Gunzenhauser, Michael G. (2002). Collaborative ethnography and the paradoxes of interpretation. *International Journal of Qualitative Studies in Education*, 15(2), 137–154.

Gewirtz, Sharon (2001). *Managerial school: Post-welfarism and social justice in education*. Florence, KY: Routledge.

Gillum, Jack & Marisol Bello (2011, March 30). When standardized test scores soared in D.C., were the gains real? *The Washington Post*.

Giroux, Henry (1994). *Disturbing pleasures: Learning popular culture*. New York: Routledge.

—(1996). *Fugitive cultures: Race, violence and youth*. New York: Routledge.

—(1997). *Channel surfing: Race talk and the destruction of today's youth*. New York: St. Martin's Press.

—(2010). *The mouse that roared: Disney and the end of innocence*. Lanham, MD: Rowman & Littlefield.

—(1991). Border pedagogy and the politics of modernism/postmodernism. *Journal of Architectural Education,* 44(2), 69–79.

—(1988). *Teachers as intellectuals: Toward a critical pedagogy of learning.* Granby, MA: Bergin & Garvey.

Giroux, Henry A. & Peter McLaren (1988). Teacher education and the politics of democratic reform, in Henry A. Giroux (ed.), *Teachers as intellectuals: Toward a critical pedagogy of learning.* Granby, MA: Bergin & Garvey, pp. 158–76.

Gordon, Jenny (2002). From Broadway to the ABCs: Making meaning of arts reform in the age of accountability. *Educational Foundations,* 16(2), 33–53.

Greene, Maxine (1988). *The dialectic of freedom.* New York: Teachers College Press.

Groves, Paula (2002). "Doesn't it feel morbid here?" High-stakes testing and the widening of the equity gap. *Educational Foundations,* 16(2), 15–31.

Gruenewald, David A. (2004). A Foucauldian analysis of environmental education: Toward the socioecological challenge of the Earth Charter. *Curriculum Inquiry,* 34(1), 71–107.

Gunzenhauser, Michael G. (1999). *Knowledge claims and ethical commitments: Toward a moral epistemology for critical ethnography in education.* (Unpublished doctoral dissertation. Chapel Hill, NC: University of North Carolina.)

— (2003). High-stakes testing and the default philosophy of education. *Theory into Practice,* 42(1), 51–8.

—(2006). Normalizing the educated subject: A Foucauldian analysis of high-stakes accountability. *Educational Studies,* 39(3), 241–59.

—(2007). Resistance as a component of educator professionalism. *Philosophical Studies in Education,* 38, 23–36.

—(2008). Care of the self in a context of accountability. *Teachers College Record,* 110(10), 2224–44.

Gunzenhauser, Michael G. & Cynthia I. Gerstl-Pepin (2002). Guest editors' introduction: The shifting context of accountability in North Carolina and the implications for arts-based reform. *Educational Foundations,* 16(2), 3–14.

Gunzenhauser, Michael G. & Andrea M. Hyde (2007). What is the value of public school accountability? *Educational Theory,* 57(4), 489–507.

Gunzenhauser, Michael G. & George W. Noblit (2001). *Reforming with the arts: Creativity in A+ classrooms and schools.* Winston-Salem, NC: Thomas S. Kenan Institute for the Arts.

—(2011). What the arts can teach school reform, in Julian Sefton-Green, Pat Thomson, Liora Bresler, & Ken Jones (eds), *The Routledge international handbook of creative learning.* London: Routledge, pp. 427–36.

Gur-Ze'ev, Ilan (ed.) (2005). *Critical theory and critical pedagogy today: Toward a new critical language in education.* Haifa, Israel: University of Haifa Faculty of Education. Retrieved from http://construct.haifa.ac.il/~ilangz/critical-pedagogy-critical-theory-today.pdf

Hamilton, Laura S., Brian M. Stecher, Julie A. Marsh, Jennifer Sloan McCombs, Abby Robyn, Jennifer Lin Russell, Scott Naftel, & Heather Barney (2007). *Standards-based accountability under No Child Left Behind: Experiences of teachers and administrators in three states.* Santa Monica, CA: RAND.

Haynes, Felicity (1998). *The ethical school: Consequences, consistency, care, ethics.* London: Routledge.

Hendrickson, Jean (2010). *From the research: An executive summary of what the research tells us.* Edmond, OK: Oklahoma A+ Schools and the University of Central Oklahoma. Retrieved from http://aplusok.org/history/reports/

Hirsch, Edward D. (1996). *Books to build on: A grade-by-grade resource guide for parents and teachers.* New York: Delta.

Hoffman, James V., Lori Czop Assaf, & Scott G. Paris (2001). High-stakes testing in reading: Today in Texas, tomorrow? *The Reading Teacher,* 54(5), 482–92.

hooks, bell (1994). *Teaching to transgress: Education as the practice of freedom.* New York: Routledge.

Hoy, David Couzens (2004). *Critical resistance: From poststructuralism to post-critique.* Cambridge, MA: MIT Press.

Hursh, David (2007). Assessing No Child Left Behind and the rise of neoliberal education policies. *American Educational Research Journal,* 44(3), 493–518.

Hyde, Andrea (2007). *Self-constitution as resistance to normalization: Agency and resistance in the era of accountability.* (Unpublished doctoral dissertation. Pittsburgh, PA: University of Pittsburgh.)

Hytten, Kathy (2010). On being wider-awake in the world, in Robert Lake (ed.), *Dear Maxine: Letters from the unfinished conversation with Maxine Greene.* New York: Teachers College Press, pp. 20–2.

Infinito, Justen (2003). Jane Elliot meets Foucault: The formation of ethical identities in the classroom. *Journal of Moral Education,* 32(1), 67–76.

Jardine, Gail M. (2005). *Foucault and education.* New York: Peter Lang.

Johnson, Craig E. (2012). *Meeting the ethical challenges of leadership: Casting light or shadow,* 4th edn. Los Angeles, CA: Sage.

Jones, Gail M., Brett D. Jones, & Tracy Y. Hargrove (2003). *The unintended consequences of high-stakes testing.* Lanham, MD: Rowman and Littlefield.

Jones, Gail M., Brett D. Jones, Belinda D. Hardin, Lisa Chapman, Tracie Yarbrough, & Marcia Davis (1999). The impact of high stakes testing on teachers and students in North Carolina. *Phi Delta Kappan,* 81(3), 199–203.

Jorgenson, Olaf & Rick Vanosdall (2002). The death of science? What we risk in our rush toward standardized testing and three R's. *Phi Delta Kappan,* 83(8), 601–5.

Kant, Immanuel (1996). *The metaphysics of morals* (Mary Gregor trans.). Cambridge, UK: Cambridge University Press. (Original work published 1797.)

King, Richard A. & Judith K. Mathers (1997). Improving schools through performance-based accountability and financial rewards. *Journal of Education Finance,* 23(2), 147–76.

Kohli, Wendy (1999). Performativity and pedagogy: The making of educational subjects. *Studies in Philosophy and Education,* 18(5), 319–26.

Kozar, Veronica F. (2011). *Accountability from the inside out: A case study of isolation and autonomy.* (Unpublished doctoral dissertation. Pittsburgh, PA: University of Pittsburgh.)

Kumashiro, Kevin (2004). *Against common sense: Teaching and learning toward social justice.* New York: Routledge Falmer.

Ladson-Billings, Gloria (2001). *Crossing over to Canaan: The journeys of new teachers in diverse classrooms.* San Francisco, CA: Jossey-Bass.

Lagemann, Ellen Condliffe (2000). *An elusive science: The troubling history of educational research.* Chicago, IL: University of Chicago Press.

Lechner, Daniel (2001). The dangerous human right to education. *Studies in Philosophy and Education,* 20(3), 279–81.

Lee, Jaekyung (2006). *Tracking achievement gaps and assessing the impact of NCLB on the gaps: An in-depth look into national and state reading and math outcome trends.* Cambridge, MA: The Civil Rights Project at Harvard University.

Levinas, Emmanuel & Seán Hand (eds) (1989). *The Levinas reader.* Oxford, UK: Blackwell.

Linn, Robert L. (2000). Assessments and accountability. *Educational Researcher,* 29(2), 4–16.

—(2005). Conflicting demands of *No Child Left Behind* and state systems: Mixed messages about school performance. *Education Policy Analysis Archives,* 13(3). Retrieved from http://epaa.asu.edu/epaa/v13n33/.

Linn, Robert L. & Carolyn Haug (2002). Stability of school-building accountability scores and gains. *Educational Evaluation and Policy Analysis,* 24(1), 29–36.

MacIntyre, Alasdair (1981). *After virtue: A study in moral theory.* Notre Dame, IN: University of Notre Dame Press.

Marshall, James D. (1996). *Michel Foucault: Personal autonomy and education.* Dordrecht, the Netherlands: Kluwer.

Marshall, James D. (2001). A critical theory of the self: Wittgenstein, Nietzsche, Foucault, *Studies in Philosophy and Education,* 20(1), 75–91.

Masschelein, Jan (2004). How to conceive of critical educational theory today? *Journal of Philosophy of Education,* 38(3), 351–67.

Masschelein, Jan & Maarten Simons (2005). The strategy of the inclusive education apparatus. *Studies in Philosophy and Education,* 24(2), 117–38.

Mathers, Judie (2004, November). Troubling the assumptions about teachers in accountability policy. (Paper presented at the annual meeting of the American Educational Studies Association. Kansas City, MO.)

Mathison, Sandra & Melissa Freeman (2003). Constraining elementary teachers' work: Dilemmas and paradoxes created by stare mandated testing. *Educational Policy Analysis Archives,* 11(34), 1–23. Retrieved from http://epaa.asu.edu/epaa/v11n34/

Mayo, Cris (1998). Foucauldian cautions on the subject and the educative implications of contingent identity, in Susan Laird (ed.), *Philosophy of Education 1997.* Urbana, IL: University of Illinois, pp. 115–23.

—(2000). The uses of Foucault. *Educational Theory,* 50(1), 103–16.

McDonough, Kevin. (1994). Overcoming ambivalence about Foucault's relevance for education, in Audrey Thompson (ed.), *Philosophy of Education 1993.* Urbana, IL: University of Illinois, pp. 86–9.

McIntyre, Alice (1997). *Making meaning of whiteness: Exploring the racial identity of white teachers.* Albany, NY: State University of New York Press.

McKinney, Monica B. (2002). Space matters: The A+ Schools Program and the ABCs of Education. *Educational Foundations,* 16(2), 77–91.

McNeil, Linda M. (2000a). Creating new inequalities: Contradictions of reform. *Phi Delta Kappan,* 81(1), 728–34.

—(2000b). Sameness, bureaucracy, and the myth of educational equity: The TAAS system of testing in Texas public schools. *Hispanic Journal of Behavioral Sciences,* 22(4), 508–23.

Meier, Deborah & George Wood (eds) (2004). *Many children left behind: How the No Child Left Behind Act is damaging our children and our schools.* Boston, MA: Beacon Press.

Mill, John Stuart (1993). *On liberty* and *Utilitarianism.* New York: Bantam Books. (Original works published 1859 and 1871, respectively.)

Mintrop, Heinrich & Tina M. Trujillo (2005). Corrective action in low-performing schools: Lessons for NCLB implementation from first-generation accountability systems. *Education Policy Analysis Archives,* 13(48). Retrieved from http://epaa.asu.edu/epaa/v13n48/

Molnar, Alex (2005). *School commercialism: From democratic ideal to market commodity.* New York: Routledge.

Murillo, Enrique G. Jr. & Susana Y. Flores (2002). Reform by shame: Managing the stigma of labels in high stakes testing. *Educational Foundations,* 16(2), 93–108.

Nash, Robert J. (2002). *"Real world" ethics: Frameworks for educators and human service professionals,* 2nd edn. New York: Teachers College Press.

Nelson, Catherine A. (2001). *Executive summary: The arts and education reform: Lessons from a four-year evaluation of the A+ Schools Program, 1995–1999.* Winston-Salem, NC: Thomas S. Kenan Institute for the Arts.

Nicholson-Goodman, JoVictoria, & Noreen B. Garman (2007). Mapping practitioner perceptions of "It's research based": Scientific discourse, speech acts and the use and abuse of research. *International Journal of Leadership in Education,* 10(3), 283–99.

Niederberger, Mary (2011, July 7). Keystone Oaks may go to 4-day week. *Pittsburgh Post-Gazette.*

Noblit, George W. & Van O. Dempsey (1996). *The social construction of virtue: Moral life in schools.* Albany, NY: State University of New York Press.

Noblit, George W., Susana Y. Flores, & Enrique G. Murillo, Jr. (eds) (2004). *Postcritical ethnography: Reinscribing critique.* Cresskill, NJ: Hampton Press.

Noblit, George W., H. Dickson Corbett, Bruce L. Wilson, & Monica B. McKinney (2009). *Creating and sustaining arts-based school reform: The A+ Schools Program.* Albany, NY: State University of New York Press.

Noddings, Nel (1984). *Caring: A feminine approach to ethics and moral education.* New York: Teachers College Press.

—(1992). *The challenge to care in schools: An alternative approach to education.* Berkeley, CA: University of California Press.

—(2007). *When school reform goes wrong.* New York: Teachers College Press.

—(2010). Maxine Greene and human freedom, in Robert Lake (ed.), *Dear Maxine: Letters from the unfinished conversation with Maxine Green.* New York: Teachers College Press, pp. xxi–xxiii.

Norris, Trevor (2011). *Consuming schools: Commercialism and the end of politics.* Toronto, Canada: University of Toronto Press.

Oakes, Jeannie, Gary Blasi, & John Rogers (2004). Accountability for adequate and equitable opportunities to learn, in Kenneth A. Sirotnik (ed.), *Holding accountability accountable: What ought to matter in public education.* New York: Teachers College Press, pp. 82–99.

Otterman, Sharon & Robert Gebeloff (2010, August 16). Triumph fades on racial gap in city schools. *The New York Times,* A1.

Otto, Stacy L. (2000). *The extreme difficulty of deciding to try: Education for the creative self.* (Unpublished doctoral dissertation. Chapel Hill, NC: University of North Carolina.)

Patterson, Jean A. (2002). Exploring reform as symbolism and expression of belief. *Educational Foundations,* 16(2), 55–75.

Paul, James L. (2005). *Introduction to the philosophies of research and criticism in education and social sciences.* Columbus, OH: Merrill/Prentice Hall.

Pignatelli, Frank (1993). What can I do? Foucault on freedom and the question of teacher agency. *Educational Theory,* 43(4), 411–32.

—(2002). Mapping the terrain of a Foucauldian ethics: A response to the surveillance of schooling. *Studies in Philosophy and Education,* 21(2), 157–80.

Popkewitz, Thomas (1991). *A political sociology of educational reform: Power/knowledge in teaching, teacher education and research.* New York: Teachers College Press.

Popkewitz, Thomas & Marie Brennan (1997). Restructuring of social and political theory in education: Foucault and a social epistemology of school practices. *Educational Theory,* 47(3), 287–313.

Popper, Karl (1963). *Conjectures and refutations: The growth of scientific knowledge.* London: Routledge & Kegan Paul.

—(1994). *The myth of the framework: In defence of science and rationality.* New York: Routledge. (Original work published 1965.)

Porter, C. Andrew, Mitchell D. Chester, & Michael D. Schlesinger (2004). Framework for an effective assessment and accountability program: The Philadelphia example, *Teachers College Record,* 106(6), 1358–400.

Postman, Neil (1995). *The end of education: Redefining the value of school.* New York: Vintage Books.

Purpel, D.E. (1989). *The moral and spiritual crisis in education: A curriculum for justice and compassion in education.* Granby, MA: Bergin & Garvey.

Raiber, Michael, Bryan Duke, Nancy Berry, Charlene Dell, & Diane Jackson (2010). *Recognizably different: Meta-analysis of Oklahoma A+ Schools.* Edmond, OK: Oklahoma A+ Schools and the University of Central Oklahoma. Retrieved from http://aplusok.org/history/reports/

Ravitch, Diane (2010). *The death and life of the great American school system: How testing and choice are undermining education.* New York: Basic Books.

Resnick, Lauren & Chris Zurawsky (2005). Getting back on course: Standards-based reform and accountability, *American Educator,* 29. Retrieved from http://www.aft.org/pubs-reports/american_educator/issues/spring05/resnick.htm.

Ricci, Carlo (2004). The case against standardized testing and the call for a revitalization of democracy. *The Review of Education, Pedagogy and Cultural Studies,* 26, 339–61.

Richardson, Joan (2009). "Quality education is our moon shot": An interview with Secretary of Education Arne Duncan. *Phi Delta Kappan,* 91(1), 24–9.

Rogers, Patricia J. (2005). Accountability, in Sandra Mathison (ed.), *Encyclopedia of evaluation.* Thousand Oaks, CA: Sage, pp. 2–4.

Rose, Mike (1989). *Lives on the boundary.* New York: Penguin Books.

—(2009). *Why school?* New York: The New Press.

Rothenberg, Paula (2000). *Invisible privilege: A memoir about race, class, and gender.* Lawrence, KS: University Press of Kansas.

Saltman, Kenneth J. (2007). *Capitalizing on disaster: Taking and breaking public schools*. Boulder, CO: Paradigm Publishers.

—(2010). *The gift of education: Public education and venture philanthropy*. New York: Palgrave Macmillan.

Sergiovanni, Thomas J. (1992). *Moral leadership: Getting to the heart of school leadership*. San Francisco, CA: Jossey-Bass.

—(1994). *Building communities in schools*. San Francisco, CA: Jossey-Bass.

Siegel, Harvey (2004). What ought to matter in public schooling: Judgment, standards, and responsible accountability, in Kenneth A. Sirotnik (ed.), *Holding accountability accountable: What ought to matter in public education*. New York: Teachers College Press, pp. 51–65.

Sirotnik, Kenneth A. (2002). Promoting responsible accountability in schools and education. *Phi Delta Kappan*, 83(9), 645–73.

—(ed.) (2004). *Holding accountability accountable: What ought to matter in public education*. New York: Teachers College Press.

Skrla, Linda & James J. Scheurich. (2001). Displacing deficit thinking in school district leadership. *Education and Urban Society*, 33(3), 235–59.

—(eds) (2004). *Educational equity and accountability: Paradigms, policies, and politics*. New York: Routledge Falmer.

Skrla, Linda, James J. Scheurich, & James Johnson (2000). *Equity-driven achievement-focused school districts*. Report. Austin, TX: Charles A. Dana Center at the University of Texas.

Smith, Mary Lee, with Linda Miller-Kahn, Walter Heinecke, & Patricia Jarvis (2004). *Political spectacle and the fate of American schools*. New York: Routledge Falmer.

St. Pierre, Elizabeth A. (2002). Science rejects post-modernism. *Educational Researcher*, 31(8), 25–7.

Starratt, Robert J. (2004). *Ethical leadership*. San Francisco, CA: Jossey-Bass.

Stecher, Brian M., Georges Vernez, & Paul Steinberg (2010). *Reauthorizing No Child Left Behind: Facts and recommendations*. Policy brief. Santa Monica, CA: RAND.

Stecher, Brian M., Scott Epstein, Laura S. Hamilton, Julie A. Marsh, Abby Robyn, Jennifer Sloan McCombs, Jennifer Russell, & Scott Naftel (2008). *Pain and gain: Implementing No Child Left Behind in three states, 2004–2006*. Santa Monica, CA: RAND.

Stengel, Barbara S. & Alan R. Tom (2006). *Moral matters: Five ways to develop the moral life of schools*. New York: Teachers College Press.

Stone, Lynda. (2005). Philosophy for educational research, in James L. Paul (ed.), *Introduction to the philosophies of research and criticism in education and the social sciences*. Upper Saddle River, NJ: Pearson, pp. 21–42.

Strike, Kenneth A. (2006). *Ethical leadership in schools: Creating community in an environment of accountability*. Thousand Oaks, CA: Corwin Press.

Sunderman, Gail L., James S. Kim, & Gary Orfield (2005). *NCLB meets school realities: Lessons from the field*. Thousand Oaks, CA: Corwin Press.

Taylor, Astra (ed.) (2009). *The examined life: Excursions with contemporary thinkers*. New York: The New Press.

Thompson, Scott (2001). The authentic standards movement and its evil twin. *Phi Delta Kappan*, 82(5), 358–62.

Todd, Sharon (2004). *Learning from the other: Levinas, psychoanalysis, and ethical possibilities in education*. Albany, NY: State University of New York Press.

Turque, Bill (2011, March 31). Rhee now concedes students' test answers may have been erased. *The Washington Post*.

Underwood, Julie (2011, July 12). ALEC exposed: Starving public schools. *The Nation*.

Valencia, Richard R. (ed.) (1997). *The evolution of deficit thinking: Educational thought and practice*. London: The Falmer Press.

Vinson, Kevin D. & E. Wayne Ross (2003). *Image and education: Teaching in the face of the new disciplinarity*. New York: Peter Lang.

Vinson, Kevin D., Rich Gibson, & E. Wayne Ross (2004). Pursuing authentic teaching in an age of standardization, in Kathleen R. Kesson & E. Wayne Ross (eds), *Defending public schools, volume II: Teaching for a democratic society*. Westport, CT: Praeger Perspectives, pp. 79–95.

Walck, Pamela E. (2011, July 7). Parents decry special ed plan. *Pittsburgh Post-Gazette*.

Weaver, Patti (2003, August 9). Judge orders teacher reinstated. *Tulsa World*, A15.

Welch, Sharon (2000). *A feminist ethic of risk*. Boulder, CO: Westview Press.

Wilson, Robert E., Michael J. Bowers, & Richard L. Hyde (2011, June 30). Untitled Report to Governor Nathan Deal of special investigation of Atlanta Public Schools Systems. (Atlanta, GA: Special Investigators, Office of the Governor.) Retrieved from http://www.courthousenews.com/2011/07/27/APS1.pdf

Zembylas, Michalinos (2003). Interrogating 'teacher identity': Emotion, resistance, and self-formation. *Educational Theory*, 53(1), 107–27.

ABOUT THE AUTHOR

Michael G. Gunzenhauser is a philosopher of education and qualitative research methodologist who studies epistemology and ethics as they relate to social justice projects in education and educational research.

He began his career as an educator at the North Carolina School of Science and Mathematics, where he was a residential counselor and residential complex coordinator for 11th and 12th grade students. In 1992, he obtained his master's degree in Higher Education and Student Affairs Administration from the University of Vermont, where he first became interested in philosophy, ethics, and education for social justice, owing in no small part to his mentors, Robert Nash and Kathleen Manning. After then coordinating precollege summer programs for Duke University's Talent Identification Program, Mike pursued his doctorate in Social Foundations of Education, also at the University of North Carolina, where mentors Lynda Stone and George Noblit and his program siblings kept him grounded in engaged scholarship, intellectual and personal relationships that continue to sustain him. In his dissertation, Mike studied the moral and epistemological grounding of critical ethnography.

Beginning in 1999, Mike was an assistant professor of Social Foundations in the Oklahoma State University College of Education, were he enjoyed a nurturing environment for his work and development as an educator and scholar. Since 2004, he has been an associate professor in the School of Education at the University of Pittsburgh. He teaches courses in philosophy of education, ethics, and research methodology in a supportive community of diverse scholar/practitioner/citizens in the Department of Administrative and Policy Studies and advises students in graduate programs in Social and Comparative Analysis in Education, School Leadership, and Higher Education Management.

In addition to articles published on high-stakes accountability policy, Mike has published articles about research methodology in *Qualitative Inquiry, International Journal of Qualitative Studies in Education,* and *Review of Higher Education.* Mike is a coeditor of *Philosophical Studies in Education* and with colleagues has guest-edited special issues of *Educational Foundations* and *Studies in Philosophy and Education.*

Mike lives outside Pittsburgh in Edgewood Borough with his dear wife, Deborah Desjardins, and their clever preschool sons, Joshua and Adam.

INDEX